STO

FRIENDS
OF ACPL

Date D...

A Maine Forest

TREES IN PROSE AND POETRY

COMPILED BY

GERTRUDE L. STONE

AND

M. GRACE FICKETT

INSTRUCTORS IN STATE NORMAL SCHOOL, GORHAM, MAINE

BOSTON, U.S.A.
GINN & COMPANY, PUBLISHERS
The Athenæum Press
1902

COPYRIGHT, 1902, BY
GERTRUDE L. STONE AND M. GRACE FICKETT

ALL RIGHTS RESERVED

TO

OUR HONORED PRINCIPAL

WILLIAM JOHNSON CORTHELL

PREFACE

TREES, in their literary aspect, have as yet found small place in the nature books of to-day; but with the increasing amount of tree study in our common schools there is need of a collection of tree stories and poems. In the compilation of this little book the aim has been to present in the form of a supplementary reader for advanced grades the best literature, legendary, historical, and fanciful, that has been inspired by our common trees.

Such a book may well have a place in every schoolroom. Where nature study is taught, the selections may be used as supplementary material; where nature study is as yet unattempted, an intelligent study of the selections must inspire the children with a love for the trees and a desire to know them better.

There is no result of nature study that does so much to transform well-known scenes as a knowledge of the trees; and an important aid to this larger vision is familiarity with the thoughts of the great writers on these most majestic specimens of the plant world.

This compilation has been made possible by the courtesy of those publishers and authors who have generously allowed the use of copyrighted material. The selections from Longfellow, Lowell, Whittier, Holmes, Hawthorne, Burroughs, Thoreau, and Aldrich have been printed by permission of and by special arrangement with Messrs. Houghton, Mifflin & Co., authorized publishers of the authors mentioned; the two poems of Bryant by permission of Messrs. D. Appleton & Co., publishers of Bryant's Complete Poetical Works; the poem of Mrs. Mace by permission of her publishers, Messrs. Damrell & Upham; while Messrs. W. J. Brier, George S. Burleigh, Madison J. Cawein, L. L. Dame, and Dr. Theodore L. Flood have kindly consented to the use of those selections which bear their names.

To these firms and individuals, for their very courteous coöperation and kindness, the sincere thanks of the compilers are most cordially extended.

G. L. S.
M. G. F.

GORHAM NORMAL SCHOOL,
    February, 1902.

CONTENTS

	PAGE
GENERAL SELECTIONS:	1
A FOREST HYMN. *William Cullen Bryant*	3
FOREST TREES. *Washington Irving*	7
APOLLO AND DAPHNE. *Tr. from Ovid*	11
THE HORSE-CHESTNUT FAMILY:	15
THE HORSE-CHESTNUT. *Philip Gilbert Hamerton*	17
FROM MY ARMCHAIR. *Henry Wadsworth Longfellow*	20
THE MAPLE FAMILY:	23
MAPLE LEAVES. *Thomas Bailey Aldrich*	25
OCTOBER COLORS. *Helen Hunt Jackson*	25
THE LEGEND OF THE MAPLE. *E. L. Ogden*	26
THE MAPLE. *James Russell Lowell*	28
THE RED MAPLE. *Henry David Thoreau*	29
MR. MAPLE AND MR. PINE. *W. J. Brier*	32
THE ROSE FAMILY:	41
I. APPLE	
THE PLANTING OF THE APPLE TREE. *William Cullen Bryant*	43
THE APPLE. *John Burroughs*	47
THE APPLE ORCHARD. *Nathaniel Hawthorne*	53
THE OLD APPLE TREE. *George Shepard Burleigh*	55
THE WAYSIDE INN. *Tr. from Johann Ludwig Uhland*	58
II. MOUNTAIN ASH	
THE LEGEND OF THE MOUNTAIN ASH	60
THE MOUNTAIN ASH. *William Wordsworth*	62
A PARABLE	63

CONTENTS

	PAGE
THE OLIVE FAMILY:	67
I. ASH	
LEGENDS OF THE ASH. *Tr. from "Deutsche Rundschau"*	69
II. OLIVE	
A PARABLE	72
THE OLIVE TREE. *Mrs. Felicia Hemans*	74
THE OLIVE TREE. *John Ruskin*	75
THE WOOD OF THE CROSS. *Tr. from "Deutsche Rundschau"*	77
THE ELM FAMILY:	79
I. ELM	
THE WASHINGTON ELM. *L. L. Dame*	81
UNDER THE WASHINGTON ELM. *Oliver Wendell Holmes*	86
SOME FAMOUS ELMS OF NEW ENGLAND. *Oliver Wendell Holmes*	89
II. MULBERRY	
THE MULBERRY TREE. *Dinah Mulock Craik*	93
THE PRIEST AND THE MULBERRY TREE. *Thomas Peacock*	96
THE BIRCH FAMILY:	99
THE BIRCH TREE. *James Russell Lowell*	101
A TASTE OF MAINE BIRCH. *John Burroughs*	104
HIAWATHA'S SAILING. *Henry Wadsworth Longfellow*	107
THE OAK FAMILY	111
THE LEGEND OF THE OAK. *Loudon*	113
THE OAK. *James Russell Lowell*	116
THE BOWDOIN OAK. *Frances L. Mace*	119
RHŒCUS. *James Russell Lowell*	123
THE BEECH FAMILY:	129
IN THE SHADOW OF THE BEECHES. *Madison J. Cawein*	131
THE BEECH TREE'S PETITION. *Thomas Campbell*	133

CONTENTS

	PAGE
THE WILLOW FAMILY:	135
I. WILLOW	
UNDER THE WILLOWS. *James Russell Lowell*	137
II. ASPEN	
THE ASPEN. *Bernhard Severin Ingemann*	139
III. POPLAR	
THE LEGEND OF THE POPLAR	142
THE SISTERS OF PHAËTHON. *Tr. from Ovid*	146
THE PINE FAMILY:	149
I. PINE	
A SONG. *Tr. from Heine*	151
PINE TREES. *John Ruskin*	152
II. FIR	
I REMEMBER, I REMEMBER. *Thomas Hood*	157
A YOUNG FIR WOOD. *Dante Gabriel Rossetti*	158
III. HEMLOCK	
THE HEMLOCK TREE. *Henry Wadsworth Longfellow*	159
MISCELLANEOUS SELECTIONS:	161
WINTER LEAFAGE. *Edith M. Thomas*	164
A PROTEST AGAINST FELLING THE TREES. *William Wordsworth*	165
CHARACTERISTICS OF THE TREES. *Edmund Spenser*	167
AMPHION. *Alfred Tennyson*	168
THE PALM TREE. *John Greenleaf Whittier*	171
GENERAL OUTLINE FOR THE STUDY OF TREES	175
HISTORICAL AMERICAN TREES	177
LIST OF SUPPLEMENTARY READING	179
NOTES	181

INDEX OF SELECTIONS

	PAGE
A Forest Hymn	3
Amphion	168
A Parable	63
A Parable	72
Apollo and Daphne	11
A Protest against felling the Trees	165
A Song	151
A Taste of Maine Birch	104
A Young Fir Wood	158
Characteristics of the Trees	167
Forest Trees	7
From my Armchair	20
Hiawatha's Sailing	107
In the Shadow of the Beeches	131
I Remember, I Remember	157
Legends of the Ash	69
Maple Leaves	25
Mr. Maple and Mr. Pine	32
October Colors	25
Pine Trees	152
Rhœcus	123
Some Famous Elms of New England	89
The Apple	47
The Apple Orchard	53
The Aspen	139
The Beech Tree's Petition	133
The Birch Tree	101
The Bowdoin Oak	119
The Hemlock Tree	159
The Horse-Chestnut	17
The Legend of the Maple	26
The Legend of the Mountain Ash	60
The Legend of the Oak	113
The Legend of the Poplar	142
The Maple	28
The Mountain Ash	62
The Mulberry Tree	93
The Oak	116
The Old Apple Tree	55
The Olive Tree	74
The Olive Tree	75
The Palm Tree	171
The Planting of the Apple Tree	43
The Priest and the Mulberry Tree	96
The Red Maple	29
The Sisters of Phaëthon	146
The Washington Elm	81
The Wayside Inn	58
The Wood of the Cross	77
Under the Washington Elm	86
Under the Willows	137
Winter Leafage	164

GENERAL SELECTIONS

One impulse from a vernal wood
May teach you more of man,
Of moral evil and of good,
Than all the sages can.

WILLIAM WORDSWORTH.

TREES IN PROSE AND POETRY

A FOREST HYMN

[ABRIDGED]

WILLIAM CULLEN BRYANT

The groves were God's first temples. Ere man learned
To hew the shaft, and lay the architrave,
And spread the roof above them, — ere he framed
The lofty vault, to gather and roll back
The sound of anthems; in the darkling wood,
Amid the cool and silence, he knelt down
And offered to the Mightiest solemn thanks
And supplication. Let me, then, at least,
Here, in the shadow of this aged wood,
Offer one hymn — thrice happy, if it find
Acceptance in His ear.

                      Father, thy hand
Hath reared these venerable columns; thou
Didst weave this verdant roof. Thou didst look down

Upon the naked earth, and, forthwith, rose
All these fair ranks of trees. They, in thy sun,
Budded, and shook their green leaves in thy breeze,
And shot toward heaven. The century-living crow,
Whose birth was in their tops, grew old and died
Among their branches, till, at last, they stood,
As now they stand, massy, and tall, and dark,
Fit shrine for humble worshiper to hold
Communion with his Maker. These dim vaults,
These winding aisles, of human pomp or pride
Report not. No fantastic carvings show
The boast of our vain race to change the form
Of thy fair works. But thou art here — thou fill'st
The solitude. Thou art in the soft winds
That run along the summit of these trees
In music; thou art in the cooler breath,
That, from the inmost darkness of the place,
Comes, scarcely felt; the barky trunks, the ground,
The fresh, moist ground, are all instinct with thee.
My heart is awed within me, when I think
Of the great miracle that still goes on,
In silence, round me — the perpetual work
Of thy creation, finished, yet renewed
Forever. Written on thy works, I read

A FOREST HYMN

The lesson of thy own eternity.
Lo! all grow old and die — but see again,
How on the faltering footsteps of decay
Youth presses — ever gay and beautiful youth,
In all its beautiful forms. These lofty trees
Wave not less proudly that their ancestors
Molder beneath them. Oh, there is not lost
One of earth's charms: upon her bosom yet,
After the flight of untold centuries,
The freshness of her far beginning lies
And yet shall lie.

Then let me often to these solitudes
Retire, and in thy presence reassure
My feeble virtue. Here its enemies,
The passions, at thy plainer footsteps shrink
And tremble and are still. O God! when thou
Dost scare the world with tempests, set on fire
The heavens with falling thunderbolts, or fill,
With all the waters of the firmament,
The swift, dark whirlwind that uproots the woods
And drowns the villages; when, at thy call,
Uprises the great deep, and throws himself
Upon the continent, and overwhelms

Its cities — who forgets not, at the sight
Of these tremendous tokens of thy power,
His pride, and lays his strifes and follies by?
Oh, from these sterner aspects of thy face
Spare me and mine, nor let us need the wrath
Of the mad unchained elements to teach
Who rules them. Be it ours to meditate,
In these calm shades, thy milder majesty,
And to the beautiful order of thy works
Learn to conform the order of our lives.

FOREST TREES

[ABRIDGED]

WASHINGTON IRVING

I HAVE paused more than once, in the wilderness of America, to contemplate the traces of some blast of wind which seemed to have rushed down from the clouds, and ripped its way through the bosom of the woodlands, — rooting up, shivering, and splintering the stoutest trees, and leaving a long track of desolation.

There is something awful in the vast havoc made among these gigantic plants; and in considering their magnificent remains, so rudely torn and mangled, hurled down to perish prematurely on their native soil, I was conscious of a strong movement of sympathy with the wood-nymphs, grieving to be dispossessed of their ancient habitations. I recollect also hearing a traveler of poetical temperament expressing the kind of horror which he felt in beholding, on the banks of the Missouri, an oak of prodigious size, which had been in a manner overpowered by an enormous wild grape-vine. The vine had clasped its huge folds round the trunk, and from thence had wound about every branch and twig, until the mighty tree had withered in its embrace. It seemed like Laocoön struggling ineffectually in the hideous coils of the monster Python. It was the lion of trees perishing in the embraces of a vegetable boa.

I am fond of listening to the conversation of English gentlemen on rural concerns, and of noticing with what taste and discrimination, and what strong, unaffected interest, they will discuss topics which in other countries are abandoned to mere woodmen or rustic cultivators. I have heard a noble earl descant on park and forest scenery with the science and feeling of a painter. He dwelt on the shape and beauty of particular trees on his estate with as much pride and technical precision as though he had been discussing the merits of statues in his collection. I found that he had gone considerable distances to examine trees which were celebrated among rural amateurs; for it seems that trees, like horses, have their established points of excellence, and that there are some in England which enjoy very extensive celebrity, from being perfect in their kind.

There is something nobly simple and pure in such a taste. It argues, I think, a sweet and generous nature to have this strong relish for the beauties of vegetation, and this friendship for the hardy and glorious sons of the forest. There is a grandeur of thought connected with this part of rural economy. It is, if I may be allowed the figure, the heroic line of husbandry. It is worthy of liberal, and freeborn, and aspiring men. He who plants an oak looks forward to future ages, and plants for posterity. Nothing can be less selfish than this. He cannot expect to sit in its shade, or enjoy its shelter; but he exults in the idea that the acorn which he has buried in the earth shall grow up into a lofty pile, and shall keep on flourishing, and increasing, and benefiting mankind, long after he shall have ceased to tread his paternal fields.

I can easily imagine the fondness and pride with which English gentlemen, of generous temperaments, but high aristocratic feelings, contemplate those magnificent trees which rise like towers and pyramids from the midst of their paternal lands. There is an affinity between all natures, animate and inanimate. The oak, in the pride and lustihood of its growth, seems to me to take its range with the lion and the eagle, and to assimilate, in the grandeur of its attributes, to heroic and intellectual man.

With its mighty pillar rising straight and direct toward heaven, bearing up its leafy honors from the impurities of earth, and supporting them aloft in free air and glorious sunshine, it is an emblem of what a true nobleman *should be:* a refuge for the weak, — a shelter for the oppressed, — a defense for the defenseless; warding off from them the peltings of the storm, or the scorching rays of arbitrary power. He who is *this,* is an ornament and a blessing to his native land. He who is *otherwise,* abuses his eminent advantages — abuses the grandeur and prosperity which he has drawn from the bosom of his country. Should tempests arise, and he be laid prostrate by the storm, who would mourn over his fall? Should he be borne down by the oppressive hand of power, who would murmur at his fate? "Why cumbereth he the ground?"

APOLLO AND DAPHNE

[Apollo, or Phœbus Apollo, was best known as god of the sun. He also had the power of healing diseases and of revealing the future. He was patron of music and poetry. In this connection read Lowell's "The Shepherd of King Admetus." Cupid had struck Apollo with an arrow which made the sun-god fall in love with Daphne, the daughter of Peneus, a river-god. Daphne, however, struck with an arrow which repelled love, paid no attention to Apollo, and attempted to escape from him.]

"IF thou but knew my name, O maiden rash,
Thou wouldst not flee, nor scorn such love as mine.
For I am not of mortal stock; my race
Is of the gods; my father Jove supreme.
An hundred temples in my honor stand —
The Delphic land and far famed Tenedos,
Ionian Claros, Lycian Patara, —
All these are subject to my sovereign sway.
The darkest secrets of the Fates are mine,
And all that was, or is, or yet shall be,
Through me alone to mortal ear is told.
My touch can make the stretchèd strings resound
In melting lays of tuneful harmony.
I am the archer god: my aim is true —

One arrow only speeds more sure than mine,
And sorely Cupid's dart hath wounded me.
To me the herbs yield all their potent juice,
And through the world men call me comforter.
But woe is me! Love's wound will not be stanched
By any potion from the choicest herb,
And these same healing arts that cure mankind
Serve not to heal their master's malady."
But Peneus' daughter paid the god no heed —
Without a word her timid flight she took,
And left him with his fair words still unsaid.
Her graceful flight enhanced her beauty's charm,
But could not yield her safety; for the god,
Urged on by love's all-powerful impulses,
In Daphne's footsteps follows hastily.
Now he is close behind; she feels his breath
Blow through her scattered hair upon her neck.
Upon her face a pallor comes; her strength
The effort of her rapid flight consumes;
And when she sees her father's waters near,
Despairingly she calls aloud for aid.
"O father, hear and bring me help! O earth,
Conceal me in thy yawning depths, or else
I pray thee, by some transformation quick,

APOLLO AND DAPHNE

Destroy this fateful beauty that I prized,
But which hath wrought so bitterly for me!"
Her prayer is scarcely done when torpor dull
Steals through her limbs with numbing heaviness.
Her yielding breast is girt with tender bark;
What was her hair is graceful leaves; her arms
Extend and change to waving branches fair.
Her foot that lately sped so swift is caught
In meshes of a sluggish, lazy root,
And last the tree-top closes round her mouth.
One charm is left; and in the leaves alone
Her beauty's glossy sheen is manifest.
But Phœbus' love unchanged remains; he grasps
With his right hand the trunk, and starts to feel
Her heart's tumultuous beating 'neath the bark.
The branches then he folds in his embrace,
And kisses wood that shrinks back from his touch.
Then spoke Apollo: "Thou my tree shalt be,
Since thou may'st never now my wife become.
Henceforth this head of mine, and this my lyre,
My quiver that I bear, thou shalt adorn
With chaplet of thy leaves, O laurel tree!
And when the Latin chiefs, with joyous song,
Shall celebrate their triumphs, when they pass

In long array beneath the Capitol,
Thou shalt be with them, and thy leaves invoke
Eternal fame on their victorious heads.
And on each side of Cæsar's palace gate,
Like silent sentinel with faithful watch,
Thou shalt protect the sacred oak between.
And as my head with unshorn locks is crowned,
Yet keeps its youthful look, so shall thy leaves
Perpetual honors speak forevermore."

From Ovid's *Metamorphoses*.

THE HORSE-CHESTNUT FAMILY

THE HORSE-CHESTNUT

PHILIP GILBERT HAMERTON

THE horse-chestnut, in the earlier weeks of May, is a sight for gods and men. If you are well outside its branches, you see the richly painted flowers rising tier above tier on all its glorious slope up to the odorous heights that belong to the birds and the bees; if you are under its shadow, you walk in a soft green light that comes through the broad spreading leaflets. No transparencies are finer than this sun-illumined canopy of green, and whilst the leaves are quite young and perfect, they are cut out so clearly as to have a grandly decorative effect. Next, as to direction of line and surface, this tree is very remarkable for its bold and decided contrasts. You have the curve of the twig, first downwards and then upwards, where it carries the flowers at its extremity. The tendency of the flowery spike itself is to be vertical, and the large leaves spread themselves out horizontally and as flatly as possible to right and left. The flowers themselves are among the very richest of spring blossoms. The coloring of the petals is made lively by the presence of white, but admirably preserved from crudity by dashes of red and yellow. When the spikes or cones of flowers are in their full splendor, the horse-chestnut reminds one of a magnificent Christmas tree, carrying a thousand lighted tapers upon its branches, but with the difference that the flowers promise life, and the renewal of life; whereas, when the pretty Christmas tapers are lighted upon a tree they are a sign that its end is near, according to Andersen's melancholy story.

The horse-chestnut has been a European tree only for the last three centuries, and is one of the happiest importations from Asia. There is an octagon of them at the Val St. Veronique, and the eight brothers are all equally well grown. Tradition says that eight boar hounds are buried under them, a hound under each tree. In the heat of summer they offer a delightful shade, for their broad leafage makes an impenetrable dome of verdure.

From *The Sylvan Year*.

A Horse-Chestnut in Blossom

FROM MY ARMCHAIR

HENRY WADSWORTH LONGFELLOW

To the Children of Cambridge, who presented to me, on my Seventy-second Birthday, February 27, 1879, this Chair, made from the Wood of the Village Blacksmith's Chestnut Tree:

Am I a king, that I should call my own
This splendid ebon throne?
Or by what reason, or what right divine,
Can I proclaim it mine?

Only, perhaps, by right divine of song
It may to me belong;
Only because the spreading chestnut tree
Of old was sung by me.

Well I remember it in all its prime,
When in the summer time
The affluent foliage of its branches made
A cavern of cool shade.

There, by the blacksmith's forge, beside the street,
Its blossoms white and sweet

Enticed the bees, until it seemed alive,
And murmured like a hive.

And when the winds of autumn, with a shout,
Tossed its great arms about,
The shining chestnuts, bursting from the sheath,
Dropped to the ground beneath.

And now some fragments of its branches bare,
Shaped as a stately chair,
Have by my hearthstone found a home at last,
And whisper of the past.

The Danish king could not in all his pride
Repel the ocean tide,
But, seated in this chair, I can in rhyme
Roll back the tide of Time.

I see again, as one in vision sees,
The blossoms and the bees,
And hear the children's voices shout and call,
And the brown chestnuts fall.

I see the smithy with its fires aglow,
I hear the bellows blow,

And the shrill hammers on the anvil beat
The iron white with heat.

And thus, dear children, have ye made for me
This day a jubilee,
And to my more than three-score years and ten
Brought back my youth again.

The heart hath its own memory, like the mind,
And in it are enshrined
The precious keepsakes, into which is wrought
The giver's loving thought.

Only your love and your remembrance could
Give life to this dead wood,
And make these branches, leafless now so long,
Blossom again in song.

THE MAPLE FAMILY

MAPLE LEAVES

THOMAS BAILEY ALDRICH

October turned my maple's leaves to gold;
The most are gone now; here and there one lingers:
Soon these will slip from out the twig's weak hold,
Like coins between a dying miser's fingers.

OCTOBER COLORS

HELEN HUNT JACKSON

The springtime holds her white and purple dear;
October, lavish, flaunts them far and near;
The summer charily her reds doth lay
Like jewels on her costliest array;
October, scornful, burns them on a bier.

From *October*.

THE LEGEND OF THE MAPLE

E. L. OGDEN

When, on the world's first harvest day,
   The forest trees before the Lord
Laid down their autumn offerings
   Of fruit, in golden sunshine stored,

The maple only, of them all,
   Before the world's great harvest king
With empty hands, and silent, stood.
   She had no offering to bring.

(For in the early summer time,
   While other trees laid by their hoard,
The maple winged her fruit with love
   And sent it daily to the Lord.)

Then ran through all the leafy wood
   A murmur and a scornful smile;
But silent still the maple stood,
   And looked, unmoved, to God the while.

And then, while fell on earth a hush
  So great it seemed like death to be,
From his white throne the mighty Lord
  Stooped down and kissed the maple tree.

At that swift kiss there sudden thrilled
  In every nerve, through every vein,
An ecstasy of joy so great
  It seemed almost akin to pain.

And then, before the forest trees,
  Blushing and pale by turns, she stood;
In every leaf, now red and gold,
  Transfigured by the kiss of God.

And still when comes the autumn time,
  And on the hills the harvest lies,
Blushing, the maple tree recalls
  Her life's one beautiful surprise.

THE MAPLE

JAMES RUSSELL LOWELL

The Maple puts her corals on in May,
While loitering frosts about the lowlands cling,
To be in tune with what the robins sing,
Plastering new log huts 'mid her branches gray;
But when the Autumn southward turns away,
Then in her veins burns most the blood of Spring,
And every leaf, intensely blossoming,
Makes the year's sunset pale the set of day.
O Youth unprescient, were it only so
With trees you plant, and in whose shade reclined,
Thinking their drifting blooms Fate's coldest snow,
You carve dear names upon the faithful rind,
Nor in that vernal stem the cross foreknow
That Age shall bear, silent, yet unresigned!

THE RED MAPLE

HENRY DAVID THOREAU

By the twenty-fifth of September the red maples generally are beginning to be ripe. . . . Some single trees, wholly bright scarlet, seen against others of their kind still freshly green, or against evergreens, are more memorable than whole groves will be by and by. How beautiful, when a whole tree is like one great scarlet fruit full of ripe juices, every leaf, from lowest limb to topmost spire, all aglow, especially if you look toward the sun! What more remarkable object can there be in the landscape? Visible for miles, too fair to be believed. If such a phenomenon occurred but once, it would be handed down by tradition to posterity, and get into the mythology at last. . . .

A small red maple has grown, perchance, far away at the head of some retired valley, a mile from any road, unobserved. It has faithfully discharged the duties of a maple there, all winter and summer, neglected none of its economies, but added to its stature in the virtue which belongs to a maple, by a steady growth for so many months, never having gone gadding abroad, and is nearer heaven than it was in the

A MAPLE TREE

spring. It has faithfully husbanded its sap, and afforded a shelter to the wandering bird; has long since ripened its seeds and committed them to the winds, and has the satisfaction of knowing, perhaps, that a thousand little well-behaved maples are already settled in life somewhere. It deserves well of mapledom. Its leaves have been asking it from time to time, in a whisper, "When shall we redden?" And now, in this month of September, this month of traveling, when men are hastening to the seaside, or the mountains, or the lakes, this modest maple, still without budging an inch, travels in its reputation, — runs up its scarlet flag on that hillside, which shows that it has finished its summer's work before all other trees, and withdraws from the contest. At the eleventh hour of the year, the tree which no scrutiny could have detected here when it was most industrious is thus, by the tint of its maturity, by its very blushes, revealed at last to the careless and distant traveler, and leads his thoughts away from the dusty road into those brave solitudes which it inhabits. It flashes out conspicuous with all the virtue and beauty of a maple, — *Acer rubrum.* We may now read its title, or *rubric,* clear. Its *virtues,* not its sins, are as scarlet.

MR. MAPLE AND MR. PINE

W. J. BRIER

ONCE upon a time, many years ago, a little maple seed, with its two gauzy wings, became lodged among the feathers of a wood pigeon, and was carried far away into the pine forest.

It fell to the ground, and the rains soon beat it into the earth. It was not sorry to get out of sight, for the Pine Family, into whose domain it had been carried, seemed displeased to see it come among them. Anyway, they all looked black and threatening to the little seed, and not at all like the trees among which it was born.

Years afterward there stood, upon the spot where the seed had fallen, a hardy tree which we can make no mistake in calling Mr. Rock Maple. In all that part of the forest Mr. Maple had no relatives. As he grew stronger and stronger, the dislike of the Pines, particularly of the Pine boys, grew likewise stronger. They begrudged him the very ground he stood on. The younger Pine boys spread out their arms to try to prevent Rock Maple from getting the light and moisture which he so much needed in that sandy soil. At times they showered great quantities of needles upon him, and at certain seasons of the year they pelted him unmercifully with their cones, — sharp, rough weapons that played havoc with Mr. Maple's garments of green, yellow, and red.

Old Mr. Pine, who waved his green head in the air nearly a hundred and fifty feet above the earth, did not seem to have very good control over his boys, for while he did not often deign to pelt Mr. Maple himself with the few cones he possessed, he never rebuked the boys for their impoliteness.

One day the boys were unusually irritable, made so by the strong wind. They knew Mr. Maple was not to blame, but there was no one else to lay the blame on, so they pelted him with cones until he lost his temper. He was just wondering what he would do to prevent the annoyance, when, looking down, he saw that some little creatures had appeared upon the scene and were striking right and left at the pines with a sharp tool against which needles and cones were of no use whatever.

"How good of those little things to take my part," said Mr. Maple to himself.

In a very short time hundreds of the Pines were lying prone upon the earth. Some were formed into a house, while others were drawn away to a small stream, were rolled into its sluggish waters, and soon disappeared forever from the gaze of Mr. Pine, who grieved for them, and of Mr. Maple, who did not.

"Nobody here now, of any consequence," exclaimed Mr. Pine, with a contemptuous look at Mr. Maple. Mr. Maple paid no attention. "If you were not such a dwarf I'd talk to you sometimes, if you *don't* amount to much," he finally said, with an air of great condescension. "It makes me hoarse to talk down so far."

For a long time after that Mr. Maple kept silent, wondering why Mr. Pine and himself had been spared.

But great surprises were in store for these two enemies. One day there came to live in the log house a family, in which was the smallest human being that the trees had ever seen,— a little girl named Camilla. She soon got into the habit of coming out and playing under the two large trees.

One day her father brought home a small box, at sight of which she went into a transport of joy, screaming, "My kit, my darling kit! I never thought to see you again!" The box was soon opened, and she lifted a queer-shaped little instrument from it; then, taking it by its long neck, she drew a small wand across it, and it gave forth a sound that thrilled both Pine and Maple.

It is too long a story to tell how both trees came to love Camilla very dearly; how delighted Mr. Pine was when she took some resin which he held out to her; how pleased Camilla looked, how white were her teeth, and how she loved him for the gift; how Mr. Maple had his reward when the frost touched him and gave him a beautiful garment, much to the delight of little Camilla, or how when the long winter was nearly done the little violinist fairly hugged him for the sugar he had yielded her.

A fatal day came at last. Men appeared with sharp axes and heavy wagons and attacked Mr. Maple. They had not cut into him very deep before one of them exclaimed to the others, "Curly maple, as I live!"

Mr. Pine laughed, but before night he had met the same fate; the man who felled him remarked to the others, "Well on to ten thousand feet in that old fellow!"

Away to a noisy place they went. Soon they were cut up into small strips by a frightful monster with very sharp teeth. These strips were carried in many different directions, some of the best pieces being loaded upon cars and hurried away to a distant city. From this place they took a long journey in the deep, dark hold of a great ship; again upon the cars, until at last they rested in a dry house.

One day one of the Maple boards and one of the Pine boards were taken out and made smooth and even on the outside.

Then a skillful workman cut them up into small pieces, and made them into curious shapes. He took pains not to leave the scratch of knife or chisel upon any of the pieces. He finally glued them all together and behold, they were of the same shape as Camilla's kit, but somewhat larger.

The man explained to an observer, "I use pine for the front, or sounding-board, as it is light and vibrant. The more porous it is the better. Maple is more dense, and is the best wood I can get for the other parts, because it is so dense, vibrates slowly, and holds the vibrations made by the pine for a long time, thus prolonging the sound."

After the slow process of finishing and varnishing was completed the violin was placed in a dark box, and there it lay for a long time.

Pine and Maple said little to each other. They were

not very comfortable nor very happy. The strings that had been stretched over them were very cruel and pressed upon the Pine, which pressed upon the sound-post, and that pressed upon the Maple. Sometimes a string broke and gave them temporary relief, but soon some one would come and put on another.

After passing through two or three stores the violin finally came to rest in a large one, in a city distant from the one in which it had been made, and all was quiet for a long time. Still Pine and Maple said but little to each other. Shut up in their dark box they didn't feel very cheerful.

"A living death, this!" grumbled Pine.

"We must make the best of it," replied Maple.

One evening a stranger came into the store and asked, "Have you a first-class violin in stock?"

"Yes, just one. I got it several months ago by the merest chance. We don't keep such instruments usually," said the dealer, taking out the violin. "It is wonderful for an instrument not ten years old."

"I want one for the evening, only," said the stranger. "Madame Camilla is here in the city, and to-night plays for the Orphans' Home. One of her violins is under treatment, and her Cremona has been broken."

"Madame Camilla!" exclaimed Pine, with a quiver of delight.

"Can it be our Camilla?" asked Maple in a trembling voice.

In a few minutes the violin was taken from its case by Camilla's own hands. She ran her fingers gently over the strings, looked at the varnish, tightened the bow and rosined it, and finally placed the violin against her shoulder, and drew the bow smoothly across the strings.

She played an air in which the coming of a storm was represented, and Pine and Maple heard once more the sighing of the wind as it swept through their branches.

"That's the sound of the wind in the pine and the maple that stood near my log cabin home when I was a little girl," said the musician to the people standing near.

Then for the first time both Pine and Maple felt certain that this was really their Camilla.

The curtain rose, the manager stepped to the front and in a few words explained the accident, and stated that a new and untried violin must be used.

"Let us lay aside all discord, and act in perfect harmony to-night," said the forgiving Maple.

"I'll do it," answered Pine, more cheerfully than he had ever spoken before.

Pine and Maple beat and throbbed under the wonderful strokes and long-drawn sweeps of the bow. When the piece was finished a storm of applause burst upon them like a tempest. Again the curtain went up and the violin found itself in the glare of the footlights once more. This time the performer touched the strings gently, and played a tune that many people who had come to the store had tried to play, the words to the first line being, "Way down upon de Swannee Ribber."

When it was finished the people were silent, and tears glistened in many eyes.

"Maple, forgive me," said the now humble Pine. "I've learned a great lesson, though a very simple one. The best results in life are accomplished through harmony and not through discord."

"We'll live in harmony hereafter," said Maple.

The great soul of the artist had breathed into the instrument and made it glorious.

THE ROSE FAMILY

    I. APPLE
   II. MOUNTAIN ASH

Lo ! sweetened with the summer light,
The full-juiced apple, waxing over-mellow,
Drops in a silent autumn night.

                          TENNYSON.

THE PLANTING OF THE APPLE TREE

WILLIAM CULLEN BRYANT

Come, let us plant the apple tree.
Cleave the tough greensward with the spade;
Wide let its hollow bed be made;
There gently lay the roots, and there
Sift the dark mold with kindly care,
   And press it o'er them tenderly,
As round the sleeping infant's feet
We softly fold the cradle-sheet;
   So plant we the apple tree.

What plant we in this apple tree?
Buds, which the breath of summer days
Shall lengthen into leafy sprays;
Boughs, where the thrush with crimson breast
Shall haunt, and sing, and hide her nest;
   We plant upon the sunny lea
A shadow for the noontide hour,
A shelter from the summer shower,
   When we plant the apple tree.

What plant we in this apple tree?
Sweets for a hundred flowery springs
To load the May-wind's restless wings,
When, from the orchard-row, he pours
Its fragrance through our open doors;
  A world of blossoms for the bee,
Flowers for the sick girl's silent room,
For the glad infant sprigs of bloom,
    We plant with the apple tree.

What plant we in this apple tree?
Fruits that shall swell in sunny June,
And redden in the August noon,
And drop when gentle airs come by
That fan the blue September sky;
  While children come, with cries of glee,
And seek them where the fragrant grass
Betrays their bed to those who pass,
    At the foot of the apple tree.

And when, above this apple tree,
The winter stars are quivering bright,
And winds go howling through the night,
Girls, whose young eyes o'erflow with mirth,

Shall peel its fruit by the cottage hearth,
  And guests in prouder homes shall see,
Heaped with the grape of Cintra's vine
And golden orange of the line,
  The fruit of the apple tree.

The fruitage of this apple tree
Winds and our flag of stripe and star
Shall bear to coasts that lie afar,
Where men shall wonder at the view
And ask in what fair groves they grew;
  And sojourners beyond the sea
Shall think of childhood's careless day
And long, long hours of summer play,
  In the shade of the apple tree.

Each year shall give this apple tree
A broader flush of roseate bloom,
A deeper maze of verdurous gloom,
And loosen, when the frost-clouds lower,
The crisp brown leaves in thicker shower;
  The years shall come and pass, but we
Shall hear no longer, where we lie,
The summer's songs, the autumn's sigh,
  In the boughs of the apple tree.

And time shall waste this apple tree.
Oh, when its aged branches throw
Thin shadows on the ground below,
Shall fraud and force and iron will
Oppress the weak and helpless still?

What shall the tasks of mercy be,
Amid the toils, the strifes, the tears
Of those who live when length of years
Is wasting this apple tree?

"Who planted this old apple tree?"
The children of that distant day
Thus to some aged man shall say;
And, gazing on its mossy stem,
The gray-haired man shall answer them:

"A poet of the land was he,
Born in the rude but good old times;
'T is said he made some quaint old rhymes
On planting the apple tree."

THE APPLE

JOHN BURROUGHS

Not a little of the sunshine of our northern winters is surely wrapped up in the apple. How could we winter over without it! How is life sweetened by its mild acids! A cellar well filled with apples is more valuable than a chamber filled with flax and wool. So much sound ruddy life to draw upon, to strike one's roots down into, as it were.

The apple is full of sugar and mucilage, which make it highly nutritious. It is said, "The operators of Cornwall, England, consider ripe apples nearly as nourishing as bread, and far more so than potatoes. In the year 1801 — which was a year of much scarcity — apples, instead of being converted into cider, were sold to the poor, and the laborers asserted that they could 'stand their work' on baked apples without meat; whereas a potato diet required either meat or some other substantial nutriment. The French and Germans use apples extensively, so do the inhabitants of all European nations. The laborers depend upon them as an article of food, and frequently make a dinner of sliced apples and bread."

Yet the English apple is a tame and insipid affair, compared with the intense, sun-colored and sun-steeped fruit our orchards yield. The best thing I know about Chile is this fact, which I learn from Darwin's *Voyage*, namely, that the apple thrives well there. Darwin saw a town there so completely buried in a wood of apple trees that its streets were merely paths in an orchard. The tree, indeed, thrives so well that large branches cut off in the spring, and planted two or three feet deep in the ground, send out roots and develop into fine, full-bearing trees by the third year. The people know the value of the apple, too. They make cider and wine of it, and then from the refuse a white and finely flavored spirit ; then by another process a sweet treacle is obtained, called honey. The children and pigs eat little or no other food. He does not add that the people are healthy and temperate, but I have no doubt they are.

The apple is the commonest and yet the most varied and beautiful of fruits. A dish of them is as becoming to the center table in winter as was the vase of flowers in the summer, — a bouquet of spitzenbergs and greenings and northern spies. A rose when it blooms, the apple is a rose when it ripens. It pleases every sense to which it can be addressed, — the touch, the smell, the sight, the taste; and when it falls in the still October days it pleases the ear. It is a call to a banquet; it is a signal that the feast is ready.

How they resist the cold! holding out almost as long as the red cheeks of the boys do. A frost that destroys the potatoes and other roots only makes the apple more crisp and vigorous; they peep out from the chance November snows unscathed. When I see the fruit vender on the street corner stamping his feet and beating his hands to keep them warm, and his naked apples lying exposed to the blasts, I wonder if they do not ache, too, to clap their hands and enliven their circulation. But they can stand it nearly as long as the vender can.

The boy is indeed the true apple eater. Just as sap draws sap, so his own juicy flesh craves the juicy flesh of the apple. His fruit-eating has little reference to the state of his appetite. Whether he be full of meat or empty of meat he wants the apple just the same. Before meal or after meal it never comes amiss. The farm boy munches apples all day long. He has nests of them in the haymow, mellowing, to which he makes frequent visits. Sometimes old Brindle, having access through the open door, smells them out and makes short work of them.

In northern mythology the giants eat apples to keep off old age. The apple is indeed the fruit of youth. As we grow old we crave apples less. It is an ominous sign. When you are ashamed to be seen eating them on the street; when you can carry them in your pocket and your hand not constantly find its way to them; when your lunch basket is without them and you can pass a winter's night by the fireside with no thought of the fruit at your elbow, — then be assured you are no longer a boy, either in heart or years.

The genuine apple eater comforts himself with an apple in its season as others with a pipe or cigar. When he has nothing else to do, or is bored, he eats an apple. While he is waiting for the train he eats an apple, sometimes several of them. When he takes a walk he arms himself with apples. His traveling bag is full of apples. He offers an apple to his companion, and takes one himself. They are his chief solace when on the road. He sows their seed all along the route. He tosses the core from the car window and from the top of the stagecoach. He would, in time, make the land one vast orchard. He dispenses with a knife. He prefers that his teeth shall have the first taste. Then he knows the best flavor is immediately beneath the skin, and that in a pared apple this is lost. If you will stew the apple, he says, instead of baking it, by all means leave the skin on. It improves the color and vastly heightens the flavor of the dish.

How the early settlers prized the apple! When their trees broke down or were split asunder by the storms, the neighbors turned out, the divided tree was put together again and fastened with iron bolts. In some of the oldest orchards one may still occasionally see a large dilapidated tree with the rusty iron bolt yet visible. Poor, sour fruit, too, but sweet in those early pioneer days.

Emerson, I believe, has spoken of the apple as the social fruit of New England. Indeed, what a promoter or abettor of social intercourse among our rural population the apple has been, — the company growing more merry and unrestrained as soon as the basket of apples was passed round. When the cider followed, the introduction and good understanding were complete.

Ours is eminently a country of the orchard. Horace Greeley said he had seen no land in which the orchard formed such a prominent feature in the rural and agricultural districts. Nearly every farmhouse in the eastern and northern states has its setting or its background of apple trees, which generally date back to the first settlement of the farm. Indeed, the orchard, more than almost any other thing, tends to soften and humanize the country, and to give the place of which it is an adjunct a settled, domestic look.

THE APPLE ORCHARD

NATHANIEL HAWTHORNE

The Old Manse! We had almost forgotten it, but we will return through the orchard. This was set out by the last clergyman, in the decline of his life, when the neighbors laughed at the hoary-headed old man for planting trees from which he could have no prospect of gathering fruit. Even had that been the case, there was only so much the better motive for planting them, in the pure and unselfish hope of benefiting his successors, — an end so seldom achieved by more ambitious efforts. But the old minister, before reaching his patriarchal age of ninety, ate the apples from this orchard during many years, and added silver and gold to his annual stipend by disposing of the superfluity. It is pleasant to think of him walking among the trees in the quiet afternoons of early autumn and picking up here and there a windfall, while he observes how heavily the branches are weighed down, and computes the number of empty flour barrels that will be filled by their burden. He loved each tree, doubtless, as if it had been his own child. An orchard has a relation to mankind, and readily connects itself with matters of the heart. The trees possess a domestic character; they have lost the wild nature of their forest kindred, and have grown humanized by receiving the care of man as well as by contributing to his wants. There is so much individuality of character, too, among apple trees that it gives them an additional claim to be the objects of human interest. One is harsh and crabbed in its manifestations; another gives us fruit as mild as charity. One is churlish and illiberal, evidently grudging the few apples that it bears; another exhausts itself in free-hearted benevolence. The variety of grotesque shapes into which apple trees contort themselves has its effect on those who get acquainted with them: they stretch out their crooked branches, and take such hold of the imagination that we remember them as humorists and odd fellows. And what is more melancholy than the old apple trees that linger about the spot where once stood a homestead, but where there is now only a ruined chimney rising out of a grassy and weed-worn cellar? They offer their fruit to every wayfarer, — apples that are bittersweet with the moral of Time's vicissitude.   From *Mosses from an Old Manse.*

THE OLD APPLE TREE

GEORGE SHEPARD BURLEIGH

A song for the brave old apple tree,
   Sturdy and hardy, a strong athlete,
   Giving a challenge to hail and sleet,
   His gray-green coat flung off at his feet,
And his stiff limbs set defiantly!

When frost would nip him, and west wind whip him,
And rain, conspiring with these, would strip him,
   In the sturdy pride of his stubborn hide
   Their wrath he has utterly defied;
   The more they raged the more he hissed;
   Each knot laid bare was a doubled fist;
   And his naked limbs could better resist
The wrestling blasts sent down to trip him!

    .   .   .   .

A strain for my gallant in garments made
By vernal sprites for his dress parade!
   Plumed with the lithest greening spray,
   The love gift of his lady May,

And wearing for this gala day
Over all his breast a bonny bouquet
In the glory of pink and pearl displayed;
Ah, now it is he is wholly gay;
His knots and gnarls are hidden away
In a scented cloud of blooms that crowd
All over his tangled head, between
The fluttering plumes of tenderest green;
And every bloom has a bee that swings
In that dainty cradle rocked by wings
Of invisible fairies hovering there;
And every bee to the blossom hums
A murmuring monody that comes
To the listening ear from everywhere,
Mixed with the odor that fills the air, —
Two dizzying sweets whose mingling seems
The genesis of nepenthe dreams;
You would think the sun had warmed the sap
In the icy veins of my gray old chap
Till his head was awhirl with the bee in his cap!

A stave for the brave in his autumn suit;
Dusty and dull from the burning sun,
And wafts from the withered fields that run;

THE OLD APPLE TREE

Yet out of the dusk of its foldings dun
How gleam the globes of his peerless fruit!
  A priceless boon, a beautiful boon,
  The jewels of Autumn's golden noon;
  Only the dream of it makes him laugh
  Into flowers, that are winnowed off like chaff,
  In the warmer air of the mid-May noon;
  Aye, while the flocks of the feathered snow
  On white wings hovering, silent, slow,
  Came down to alight on his naked breast,
  In his old heart quivered a sweet unrest,
  The prescience of his own bloom shower,
  And this crowning wealth of his leafy bower.

Then a song for the brave old apple tree,
  For his lavish bounty, and gallant show,
  And his tough old fibers that tougher grow
  In the storm's insult, and the smothering snow!
Ah, well for our hearts were they brave as he!

THE WAYSIDE INN

I halted at a pleasant inn,
   As I my way was wending —
A golden apple was the sign,
   From knotty bough depending.

Mine host — it was an apple tree —
   He smilingly received me,
And spread his sweetest, choicest fruit
   To strengthen and relieve me.

Full many a little feathered guest
   Came through his branches springing;
They hopped and flew from spray to spray,
   Their notes of gladness singing.

Beneath his shade I laid me down,
   And slumber sweet possessed me;
The soft wind blowing through the leaves
   With whispers low caressed me.

"Mine host — it was an apple tree"

And when I rose and would have paid
  My host so open-hearted,
He only shook his lofty head —
  I blessed him and departed.

              Translated from Johann Ludwig Uhland.

THE LEGEND OF THE MOUNTAIN ASH

It was gone and nobody had any clew to its whereabouts. Specially hard it was, too, to lose the wonderful golden cup just before one of the great feasts of the gods. All Olympus talked and wondered, until the bird of Jupiter chanced to hear Hebe, the lovely cup-bearer, mourn the loss.

"The golden cup lost? Oh, no," the eagle declared. "That is what I saw only an hour past when I was in swift flight over the earth. It is in a cave of Earth and it is guarded by demons. Grant me the privilege and it shall be my part to find the cave again and bring back the cup to Olympus."

Permission was asked of Jupiter; he nodded assent. Strong in talon, keen of eye, swift in flight, what better messenger could be sent than the eagle?

Straightway he started on his errand. Soon the cave was found again, but the demons refused to give up their prize and a fierce struggle began. The eagle was one against many, but he had promised to bring back the cup, and he resolved to fulfill his promise or forfeit his life.

THE LEGEND OF THE MOUNTAIN ASH

The eagle made attack after attack. Again and again the demons drove him back from the mouth of the cave. The arrows they hurled after him drew many a drop of blood and caused many a feather to fall to the ground. It seemed to the exulting demons that the noble bird had lost the battle, when with a swift drop, and then the magnificent upward swoop that only the eagle can make, the shining trophy was caught in the strong talons of the bird and carried high into the heavens.

The gods rejoiced in the return of the cup, and did high honor to its winner. Earth also had reason to be glad over the struggle; for wherever the blood of the eagle dropped and the feathers fell, there sprang up a beautiful tree with feather-like leaves and blood-red berries. Every autumn, even to this day, do the mountain ash trees hang out their red badge of the courage of the eagle.

THE MOUNTAIN ASH

WILLIAM WORDSWORTH

      The mountain ash
No eye can overlook, when 'mid a grove
Of yet unfaded trees she lifts her head
Decked with autumnal berries, that outshine
Spring's richest blossoms; and ye may have marked,
By a brookside or solitary tarn,
How she her station doth adorn;—the pool
Glows at her feet, and all the gloomy rocks
Are brightened round her.

From The Excursion.

A PARABLE

[Although from its name the pomegranate should fall in the rose family, the peculiar structure of the fruit has caused most botanists to place it in a family by itself.]

One day in spring, Solomon, then a youth, sat under the palm trees in the garden of the king, his father, with his eyes fixed on the ground, and absorbed in thought.

Nathan, his preceptor, went up to him, and said, "Why sittest thou thus, musing under the palm trees?"

The youth raised his head, and answered, "Nathan, I am very desirous to behold a miracle."

"A wish," said the prophet, with a smile, "that I had myself when I was young."

"And was it granted?" hastily asked the prince.

"A man of God," answered Nathan, "came to me, bringing in his hand a pomegranate seed. 'Observe,' said he, 'what this seed will turn to!' He then made a hole in the earth, and put the seed into the hole and covered it. Scarcely had he drawn back his hand, when the earth parted, and I saw two small leaves shoot forth. But no sooner did I perceive them than the leaves separated, and from between them rose a round stem, covered with bark; and the stem became every moment higher and thicker.

"The man of God then said to me, 'Take notice.' And while I was looking, seven shoots issued from the stem, like the seven branches on the candlestick of the altar. I was amazed, but the man of God bade me be silent, and attend. 'Behold,' said he, 'new creations will soon make their appearance.'

"He then brought water in the hollow of his hand, from the stream which flowed past, and lo! all the branches were covered with green leaves, so that a cooling shade was thrown around us, together with a delicious odor. 'Whence,' said I, 'is this perfume amid the refreshing shade?' 'Seest thou not,' said the man of God, 'the scarlet blossom, as, shooting forth from among the green leaves, it hangs down in clusters?'

"I was about to answer, when a gentle breeze played in the leaves, and strewed the blossoms around us, as the autumnal blast scatters the withered foliage. No sooner had the blossoms fallen than the red pomegranates appeared suspended among the leaves, like almonds on the staves of Aaron. The man of God then left me in profound amazement."

Nathan ceased speaking. "What is the name of the godlike man?" asked Solomon, hastily. "Doth he yet live? Where doth he dwell?"

"Son of David," replied Nathan, "I have related to thee a vision."

When Solomon heard these words, he was troubled in his heart, and said, "How canst thou deceive me thus?"

"I have not deceived thee, son of David," rejoined Nathan. "Behold, in thy father's garden thou may'st see all that I have told thee. Doth not the same thing take place with every pomegranate, and with other trees?"

"Yes," said Solomon, "but by degrees, and in a long time."

Then Nathan answered, "Is it therefore the less a divine work, because it takes place slowly and silently? There are no miracles that do not proceed from God. When he reveals himself only in the ordinary course of nature, we do not fully realize that he is the sole source of all we witness. It is only when he reveals his power in manifestations not in the ordinary course of nature that we cry, 'A miracle!' If that which is now so familiar because it is so constant, were rare or occasional, we should then see in every manifestation of divine power an actual miracle."

THE OLIVE FAMILY

I. ASH
II. OLIVE

If the oak precede the ash,
We shall have both rain and splash;
If the ash precede the oak,
We shall have both fire and smoke;
But if they both come out together
We shall then have lovely weather.

OLD RHYME.

LEGENDS OF THE ASH

DR. FERD. ADALB. JUNKER VON LANGEGG

LIKE the oak, the ash was an object of high veneration with the Celts and Germans, but especially with the Scandinavian races, in whose religious myths this tree took a prominent part. The Northern people valued the sacred ash as the symbol of the universe. Always young and dew-besprinkled, it connects Heaven, Earth, and Hell, and has three roots, one of which leads to the home of the gods, one to the abode of the giants, the other to the regions of darkness and cold. Under each root is a wonderful spring; each spring is sacred and gives a yellow color to all it touches. At the first spring sit the three destinies who hold judgment, and who each day draw water to pour on the branches of the ash. A wise man guards the second spring. From the ash falls bee-nourishing dew, called the fall of the honey. On the branches and the roots sit and spring a variety of animals, — an eagle, a squirrel, four harts, and a snake. The eagle is subtile and wise, sits on the tree top, and between his eyes sits the hawk, friend of the eagle. The snake lies at the third spring, which feeds it, and the squirrel vanishes up and down the tree and seeks to excite a quarrel. At last Surtur burned down the tree, yet it was renewed fresh and green, and the gods assembled as before under its branches.

The ash, which the scalds chose as a tree symbolic of the universe, is found farther north than the oak. It is the most abundant tree beyond the Baltic, and its wood served for many purposes for which the pine trees of the North were not suitable. The saga heroes fashioned their long spear handles and ax hafts from ash wood, from which also they usually built their boats. This may have been the reason why the learned Bishop Adam of Bremen, who lived in the eleventh century, calls the Danish and Norwegian vikings Aschmen (ashmen), or because, as the Edda narrates, the first man was fashioned from a block of ash.

The Edda relates that the universe tree was the sacred ash. Though an ash, yet it was an evergreen tree, and there were many sacred trees scattered over all northern Europe which remained green summer and winter, and were highly esteemed. According to the account of Adam von Bremen such a tree stood before a great temple in Upsala; and in Ditmarsh, carefully hedged in, was a similarly honored tree, which was bound with the destiny of the land in a mystic manner. When Ditmarsh lost her freedom, the tree withered. But a magpie, one of the most distinguished birds of omen of the North, came and nested on it, and brooded five all white young ones, a sign that the land would one day win back its freedom.

In contradiction to the old adage, according to which the roots of the sacred ash were half destroyed by snakes, the leaves and the wood of the ash in northern Europe were considered a mighty protection against snakes and other vermin. It is related that the serpent's antipathy for the ash was so great that, once enclosed by a circle drawn with an ash stick, he was doomed to remain forever within that circle.

Translated from *Deutsche Rundschau*.

A PARABLE

And when they told it to Jotham, he went and stood in the top of Mount Gerizim, and lifted up his voice, and cried, and said unto them, "Hearken unto me, ye men of Shechem, that God may hearken unto you.

"The trees went forth on a time to anoint a king over them; and they said unto the olive tree, 'Reign thou over us.'

"But the olive tree said unto them, 'Should I leave my fatness, wherewith by me they honor God and man, and go to be promoted over the trees?'

"And the trees said to the fig tree, 'Come thou, and reign over us.'

"But the fig tree said unto them, 'Should I forsake my sweetness, and my good fruit, and go to be promoted over the trees?'

"Then said the trees unto the vine, 'Come thou, and reign over us.'

"And the vine said unto them, 'Should I leave my wine, which cheereth God and man, and go to be promoted over the trees?'

A PARABLE

"Then said all the trees unto the bramble, 'Come thou, and reign over us.'

"And the bramble said unto the trees, 'If in truth ye anoint me king over you, then come and put your trust in my shadow: and if not, let fire come out of the bramble, and devour the cedars of Lebanon.'"

From the *Bible*, Book of Judges, chap. ix.

THE OLIVE TREE

MRS. FELICIA HEMANS

THE palm — the vine — the cedar — each hath power
To bid fair Oriental shapes glance by,
And each quick glistening of the laurel bower
Wafts Grecian images o'er fancy's eye.
But thou, pale Olive! — in thy branches lie
Far deeper spells than prophet-grove of old
Might e'er enshrine: — I could not hear thee sigh
To the wind's faintest whisper, nor behold
One shiver of thy leaves' dim silvery green,
Without high thoughts and solemn, of that scene
When, in the garden, the Redeemer pray'd —
When pale stars look'd upon his fainting head,
And angels, ministering in silent dread,
Trembled, perchance, within thy trembling shade.

THE OLIVE TREE

JOHN RUSKIN

I CHALLENGE the untraveled English reader to tell me what an olive tree is like.

I know he cannot answer my challenge. He has no more idea of an olive tree than if olives grew only in the fixed stars. Let him meditate a little on this one fact, and consider its strangeness, and what a willful and constant closing of the eyes to the most important truths it indicates on the part of the modern artist. Observe, a want of perception, not of science. I do not want painters to tell me any scientific facts about olive trees. But it had been well for them to have felt and seen the olive tree; to have loved it for Christ's sake, partly also for the helmed Wisdom's sake which was to the heathen in some sort as that nobler Wisdom which stood at God's right hand, when He founded the earth and established the heavens. To have loved it even to the hoary dimness of its delicate foliage, subdued and faint of hue, as if the ashes of the Gethsemane agony had been cast upon it forever; and to have traced, line for line, the gnarled writhings of its intricate branches, inlaid on the blue field of the sky, and the small, rosy-white stars of its spring blossoming, and the beads of sable fruit scattered by autumn along its topmost boughs, — the right, in Israel, of the stranger, the fatherless, and the widow, — and, more than all, the softness of the mantle, silver-gray, and tender like the down on a bird's breast, with which, far away, it veils the undulation of the mountains; these it had been well for them to have seen and drawn, whatever they had left unstudied in the gallery.

THE WOOD OF THE CROSS

FERD. ADALB. JUNKER VON LANGEGG

In the early Middle Ages it was believed that there were four kinds of wood in the cross. "The cross was made of palm, cedar, cypress, and olive."

The Venerable Bede constructed the cross of four kinds of wood, the beam of cypress, the arms of cedar, the headpiece of fir, and the footpiece of boxwood. According to the apocryphal gospel of Nicodemus the cross was made from the palm and the olive fastened together, — a plan which was considered orthodox. Costly crucifixes were made in this way. The godly Chrysostom recognized only three varieties of wood, quoting from Isaiah as authority: "The glory of Lebanon shall come unto thee, the fir tree, the pine tree, and the box together, to beautify the place of my sanctuary; and I will make the place of my feet glorious."

Out of what kind of wood the cross actually was made must remain an open question. We can accept the testimony of Lepsius that in his time the pieces of wood which were exhibited as relics of the cross were of oak. He writes, "Of what was the cross made? Necessarily of a common wood lying close at hand. Of what was that of our Savior? We think it was of oak, first, because trustworthy men pronounce the little pieces of holy wood which exist to-day to be of that kind of wood; second, because that tree was common in Judea and still is so; third, because its wood was strong and adapted to burdens."

The legend which mentions the trembling poplar as the tree from which the cross was made, and whose leaves since that time have never stood still, is of earlier origin and is confined to limited districts. This trembling, so it is said in many parts of Germany, is the punishment of the tree for its pride. It refused to bow before the Lord, as all other trees did reverentially, when at one time He wandered through the northern forests. This legend recalls the wonderful palm in the apocryphal gospel of the child Jesus, which refused the crown in order to offer its fruit to the Virgin when she rested under its shadow, and which was rewarded by the Holy Child with the words: "Lift thy head, O Palm, and be the companion of the trees which are in the Paradise of my Father."

Translated from *Deutsche Rundschau.*

THE ELM FAMILY

I. ELM
II. MULBERRY

THE WASHINGTON ELM

[ABRIDGED]

L. L. DAME

AT the north end of the Common in Old Cambridge stands the famous Washington Elm, the most famous of American trees. It is of goodly proportions, but as far as girth of trunk and spread of branches constitute the claim upon our respect, there are many nobler specimens of the American elm in historic Middlesex.

Extravagant claims have been made with regard to its age, but it is extremely improbable that any tree of this species has ever rounded out its third century. When Governor Winthrop and Lieutenant-Governor Dudley, in 1630, rode along the banks of the Charles in quest of a suitable site for the capital of their colony, it is barely possible that the great elm was in being. The life of the tree, however, probably does not date farther back than the last quarter of the seventeenth century. In its early history there was nothing to distinguish it from its peers of the greenwood. When the surrounding forest fell beneath the ax of the woodman, the trees conspicuous for size and beauty escaped the general destruction; among these was the Washington Elm; but there is no evidence that it surpassed its companions.

But when troublous times came, and the murmurings of discontent were voicing themselves in more and more articulate phrase, the old tree must have been privy to a good deal of treasonable talk — at first whispered, with many misgivings, under the cover of darkness: later, in broad daylight, fearlessly spoken aloud. The smoke of bonfires, in which blazed the futile proclamations of the king, was wafted through its branches. It saw the hasty burial, by night, of the Cambridge men who were slain upon the nineteenth of April, 1775; it saw the straggling arrival of the beaten, but not disheartened, survivors of Bunker Hill; it saw the Common — granted to the town as a training field — suddenly transformed to a camp, under General Artemas Ward, commander-in-chief of the Massachusetts troops.

The crowning glory in the life of the great elm was at hand. On the twenty-first of June, Washington, without allowing himself time to take leave of his family, set out on horseback from Philadelphia, arriving

THE WASHINGTON ELM

at Cambridge on the second of July. Sprightly Dorothy Dudley in her Journal describes the exercises of the third with the florid eloquence of youth.

"To-day, he [Washington] formally took command, under one of the grand old elms on the Common. It was a magnificent sight. The majestic figure of the General, mounted upon his horse beneath the wide-spreading branches of the patriarch tree; the multitude thronging the plain around, and the houses filled with interested spectators of the scene, while the air rung with shouts of enthusiastic welcome, as he drew his sword, and thus declared himself Commander-in-chief of the Continental Army."

Great events which mark epochs in history bestow an imperishable dignity even upon the meanest objects with which they are associated. When Washington drew his sword beneath the branches, the great elm, thus distinguished above its fellows, passed at once into history, henceforward to be known as the Washington Elm.

> Under the brave old tree
> Our fathers gathered in arms, and swore
> They would follow the sign their banners bore,
> And fight till the land was free.

The elm was often honored by the presence of Washington, who, it is said, had a platform built among the branches, where, we may suppose, he used to ponder over the plans of the campaign. The Continental Army, born within the shade of the old tree, overflowing the Common, converted Cambridge into a fortified camp. Here, too, the flag of thirteen stripes for the first time swung to the breeze.

These were the palmy days of the elm. When the tide of war set away from New England, the Washington Elm fell into unmerited neglect. The struggling patriots had no time for sentiment; and when the war came to an end they were too busy in shaping the conduct of the government, and in repairing their shattered fortunes, to pay much attention to trees. It was not until the great actors in those days were rapidly passing away that their descendants turned with an affectionate regard to the enduring monuments inseparably associated with the fathers.

On the third of July, 1875, the citizens of Cambridge celebrated the one hundredth anniversary of Washington's assuming command of the army. The old tree was the central figure of the occasion. The American flag floated above the topmost branches, and a profusion of smaller flags waved amid the foliage. Never tree received a more enthusiastic ovation.

It is inclosed by a circular iron fence erected by the Reverend Daniel Austin. Outside the fence, but under the branches, stands a granite tablet erected by the city of Cambridge, upon which is cut an inscription written by Longfellow:

> UNDER THIS TREE
> WASHINGTON
> FIRST TOOK COMMAND
> OF THE
> AMERICAN ARMY,
> JULY 3D, 1775.

Never has tree been cherished with greater care, but its days are numbered. A few years more or less, and, like Penn's Treaty Elm and the famous Charter Oak, it will be numbered with the things that were.

UNDER THE WASHINGTON ELM, CAMBRIDGE

OLIVER WENDELL HOLMES

(APRIL 27, 1861)

EIGHTY years have passed, and more,
   Since under the brave old tree
Our fathers gathered in arms, and swore
They would follow the sign their banners bore,
   And fight till the land was free.

Half of their work was done,
   Half is left to do, —
Cambridge, and Concord, and Lexington!
When the battle is fought and won,
   What shall be told of you?

Hark! — 't is the south-wind moans, —
   Who are the martyrs down?
Ah, the marrow was true in your children's bones
That sprinkled with blood the cursèd stones
   Of the murder-haunted town!

THE WASHINGTON ELM

What if the storm-clouds blow?
   What if the green leaves fall?
Better the crashing tempest's throe
Than the army of worms that gnawed below;
   Trample them one and all!

Then, when the battle is won,
   And the land from traitors free,
Our children shall tell of the strife begun
When Liberty's second April sun
   Was bright on our brave old tree!

SOME FAMOUS ELMS OF NEW ENGLAND

OLIVER WENDELL HOLMES

Don't you want to hear me talk trees a little now? That is one of my specialties.

I shall speak of trees as we see them, love them, adore them in the fields, where they are alive, holding their green sunshades over our heads, talking to us with their hundred thousand whispering tongues, looking down on us with that sweet meekness which belongs to huge, but limited organisms,— which one sees in the brown eyes of oxen, but most in the patient posture, the outstretched arms, and the heavy drooping robes of these vast beings endowed with life, but not with soul, — which outgrow us and outlive us, but stand helpless, — poor things! — while Nature dresses and undresses them, like so many full-sized but underwitted children.

There is a mother idea in each particular kind of tree, which, if well marked, is probably embodied in the poetry of every language. Take the oak, for instance, and we find it always standing as a type of strength and endurance. I wonder if you ever thought of the single mark of supremacy which distinguishes this tree from those around it? The others shirk the work of resisting gravity; the oak alone defies it. It chooses the horizontal direction for its limbs so that their whole weight may tell, and then stretches them out fifty or sixty feet, so that the strain may be mighty enough to be worth resisting. You will find that, in passing from the extreme downward droop of the branches of the weeping willow to the extreme upward inclination of those of the poplar, they sweep nearly half a circle. At 90° the oak stops short; to slant upward another degree would mark infirmity of purpose; to bend downwards, weakness of organization. The American elm betrays something of both, yet sometimes, as we shall see, puts on a certain resemblance to its sturdier neighbor.

I shall never forget my ride and my introduction to the great Johnston elm. As I rode along the pleasant way, watching eagerly for the object of my journey, the rounded tops of the elms rose from time to time at the roadside. Wherever one looked taller and fuller than the rest, I asked myself, "Is this it?" But as I drew nearer, they grew smaller, — or it proved, perhaps, that two standing in a line had looked like one, and so deceived me. At last, all at once, when I was not thinking of it, — I declare to you it makes my flesh creep when I think of it now, — all at once I saw a great green cloud swelling in the horizon, so vast, so symmetrical, of such Olympian majesty and imperial supremacy among the lesser forest growths, that my heart stopped short, then jumped at my ribs as a hunter springs at a five-barred gate, and I felt all through me, without need of uttering the words, "This is it!"

You will find this tree described, with many others, in the excellent Report upon the Trees and Shrubs of Massachusetts. It is a grand elm for size of trunk, spread of limbs, and muscular development,—one of the first, perhaps the first, of the first class of New England elms.

The largest actual girth I have ever found at five feet from the ground is in the great elm lying a stone's throw or two north of the main road (if my points of compass are right) in Springfield. But this has much the appearance of having been formed by the union of two trunks growing side by side.

The West Springfield elm and one upon Northampton meadows belong also to the first class of trees.

There is a noble old wreck of an elm at Hatfield, which used to spread its claws out over a circumference of thirty-five feet or more before they covered the foot of its bole up with earth. This is the American elm most like an oak of any I have ever seen.

The Sheffield elm is equally remarkable for size and perfection of form. I have seen nothing that comes near it in Berkshire County, and few to compare with it anywhere. I am not sure that I remember any other first-class elms in New England, but there may be many.

From *The Autocrat of the Breakfast-Table.*

THE MULBERRY TREE

DINAH MULOCK CRAIK

When the long hot days are nearly gone,
And the fields lie misty in early dawn,
And the spiderwebs hang from blade to blade,
Heavy with rain and dun with shade,
Till the lazy sun rises late from his bed,
Large and solemn and round and red,
And changes them all into diamonds bright,
Like common things, glorified in love's light,—
> Oh, then is the prime, the golden prime,
> Of the patient mulberry tree!

Oh, the mulberry tree is of trees the queen!
Bare long after the rest are green:
But as time steals onwards, while none perceives
Slowly she clothes herself with leaves —
Hides her fruit under them, hard to find,
And, being a tree of steadfast mind,
Makes no show of blossom or berry,

Lures not a bird to come and make merry
> Under her boughs, her dark rough boughs —
> The prudent mulberry tree.

But by and by, when the flowers grow few
And the fruits are dwindling and small to view —
Out she comes in her matron grace
With the purple myriads of her race:
Full of plenty from root to crown,
Showering plenty her feet adown,
While far overhead hang gorgeously
Large luscious berries of sanguine dye,
> For the best grows highest, always highest,
> Upon the mulberry tree!

And so she lives through her fruitful season,
Fairest tree that blows summer breeze on; —
Till the breeze sharpens to fierce wind cold,
And the sun himself sickens, worn and old,
And sudden frosts the green lawn cover
And the day of the mulberry tree is over.
Her half-ripe treasures strew all the grass
Or wither greenly aloft. We pass
> Like summer friends when her beauty ends.
> Not a sigh for the mulberry tree!

THE MULBERRY TREE 95

Yet stands she in the October sun,
Her fruits departed — her joys all done,
And lets the wind rave through her emptied boughs
Like a mother left lone in a childless house;
Till, some still night under frosty skies,
She drops her green clothing off — and dies:
Without a blight or mildew to taint,
Uncomplaining as some sweet saint
    Who, her full life past, dies, calm to the last —
    The grand old mulberry tree!

THE PRIEST AND THE MULBERRY TREE

THOMAS L. PEACOCK

Did you hear of the curate who mounted his mare,
And merrily trotted along to the fair?
Of creature more tractable none ever heard.
In the height of her speed she would stop at a word;
But again, with a word, when the curate said "Hey,"
She put forth her mettle and galloped away.

As near to the gates of the city he rode,
While the sun of September all brilliantly glowed,
The good priest discovered, with eyes of desire,
A mulberry tree in a hedge of wild brier;
On boughs long and lofty, in many a green shoot,
Hung, large, black, and glossy, the beautiful fruit.

The curate was hungry and thirsty to boot;
He shrunk from the thorns, though he longed for the fruit;
With a word he arrested his courser's keen speed,
And he stood up erect on the back of his steed;

THE PRIEST AND THE MULBERRY TREE 97

On the saddle he stood while the creature stood still,
And he gathered the fruit till he took his good fill.

"Sure, never," he thought, "was a creature so rare,
So docile, so true, as my excellent mare;
Lo, here now I stand," and he gazed all around,
"As safe and as steady as if on the ground;
Yet how had it been, if some traveler this way
Had, dreaming no mischief, but chanced to cry 'Hey'?"

He stood with his head in the mulberry tree,
And he spoke out aloud in his fond reverie;
At the sound of the word the good mare made a push,
And down went the priest in the wild brier bush.
He remembered too late, on his thorny green bed,
Much that well may be thought cannot wisely be said.

THE BIRCH FAMILY

THE BIRCH TREE

JAMES RUSSELL LOWELL

Rippling through thy branches goes the sunshine,
Among thy leaves that palpitate forever;
Ovid in thee a pining Nymph had prisoned,
The soul once of some tremulous inland river,
Quivering to tell her woe, but, ah! dumb, dumb forever!

While all the forest, witched with slumberous moonshine,
Holds up its leaves in happy, happy stillness,
Waiting the dew, with breath and pulse suspended,
I hear afar thy whispering, gleamy islands,
And track thee wakeful still amid the wide-hung silence.

On the brink of some wood-nestled lakelet,
Thy foliage, like the tresses of a Dryad,
Dripping round thy slim white stem, whose shadow
Slopes quivering down the water's dusky quiet,
Thou shrink'st as on her bath's edge would some startled Naiad.

Thou art the go-between of rustic lovers;
Thy white bark has their secrets in its keeping;
Reuben writes here the happy name of Patience,
And thy lithe boughs hang murmuring and weeping
Above her, as she steals the mystery from thy keeping.

Thou art to me like my belovèd maiden,
So frankly coy, so full of trembly confidences;
Thy shadow scarce seems shade, thy pattering leaflets
Sprinkle their gathered sunshine o'er my senses,
And Nature gives me all her summer confidences.

Whether my heart with hope or sorrow tremble,
Thou sympathizest still; wild and unquiet,
I fling me down; thy ripple, like a river,
Flows valleyward, where calmness is, and by it
My heart is floated down into the land of quiet.

TRUNK OF PAPER BIRCH

A TASTE OF MAINE BIRCH

JOHN BURROUGHS

I READ in Gibbon that the natives of ancient Assyria used to celebrate in verse or prose the three hundred and sixty uses to which the various parts and products of the palm tree were applied. The Maine birch is turned to so many accounts that it may well be called the palm of this region. Uncle Nathan, our guide, said it was made especially for the camper-out; yes, and for the woodman and frontiersman generally. It is a magazine, a furnishing store set up in the wilderness, whose goods are free to every comer. The whole equipment of the camp lies folded in it and comes forth at the beck of the woodman's ax; tent, waterproof roof, boat, camp utensils, buckets, cups, plates, spoons, napkins, tablecloths, paper for letters or for your journal, torches, candles, kindling wood and fuel. The canoe-birch yields you its vestments with the utmost liberality. Ask for its coat, and it gives you its waistcoat also. Its bark seems wrapped about it layer on layer and comes off with great ease. We saw many rude structures and cabins shingled and sided with it, and haystacks capped with it.

Near a maple-sugar camp there was a large pile of birch-bark sap buckets, — each bucket made of a piece of bark about a yard square, folded up as the tinman folds up a sheet of tin to make a square vessel, the corners bent around against the sides and held by a wooden pin. When, one day, we were overtaken by a shower in traveling through the woods, our guide quickly stripped large sheets of the bark from a near tree, and we had each a perfect umbrella as by magic. When the rain was over, and we moved on, I wrapped mine about me like a large leather apron, and it shielded my clothes from the wet bushes. When we came to a spring, Uncle Nathan would have a birch-bark cup ready before any of us could get a tin one out of his knapsack, and I think water never tasted so sweet as from one of these bark cups. It is exactly the thing. It just fits the mouth, and it seems to give new virtues to the water. It makes me thirsty now when I think of it. In camp Uncle Nathan often drank his tea and coffee from a bark cup; the china closet in the birch tree was always handy, and our vulgar tinware was generally a good deal mixed, and the kitchen maid not at all particular about dish-washing. We all tried the oatmeal with the maple syrup in one of these dishes, and the stewed mountain cranberries, using a birch-bark spoon, and never found service better. Uncle Nathan declared he could boil potatoes in a bark kettle, and I did not doubt him. Instead of sending our soiled napkins and table spreads to the wash, we rolled them up into candles and torches, and drew daily upon our stores in the forest for new ones. But the great triumph of the birch is, of course, the bark canoe. The design of a savage, it yet looks like the thought of a poet; and its grace and fitness haunt the imagination. I suppose its production was the inevitable result of the Indians' wants and surroundings, but that does not detract from its beauty. It is, indeed, one of the fairest flowers the thorny plant of necessity ever bore.

HIAWATHA'S SAILING

HENRY WADSWORTH LONGFELLOW

"GIVE me of your bark, O Birch Tree!
Of your yellow bark, O Birch Tree!
Growing by the rushing river,
Tall and stately in the valley!
I a light canoe will build me,
Build a swift Cheemaun for sailing,
That shall float upon the river
Like a yellow leaf in Autumn,
Like a yellow water lily!

"Lay aside your cloak, O Birch Tree!
Lay aside your white-skin wrapper,
For the Summer-time is coming,
And the sun is warm in heaven,
And you need no white-skin wrapper!"

Thus aloud cried Hiawatha
In the solitary forest,
By the rushing Taquamenaw,
When the birds were singing gayly,
In the Moon of Leaves were singing,

And the sun, from sleep awaking,
Started up and said, "Behold me!
Gheezis, the great Sun, behold me!"

And the tree with all its branches
Rustled in the breeze of morning,
Saying, with a sigh of patience,
"Take my cloak, O Hiawatha!"

With his knife the tree he girdled;
Just beneath its lowest branches,
Just above the roots, he cut it,
Till the sap came oozing outward;
Down the trunk, from top to bottom,
Sheer he cleft the bark asunder,
With a wooden wedge he raised it,
Stripped it from the trunk unbroken.

"Give me of your boughs, O Cedar!
Of your strong and pliant branches,
My canoe to make more steady,
Make more strong and firm beneath me!"

Through the summit of the Cedar
Went a sound, a cry of horror,
Went a murmur of resistance;
But it whispered, bending downward,
"Take my boughs, O Hiawatha!"

HIAWATHA'S SAILING

Down he hewed the boughs of cedar,
Shaped them straightway to a framework,
Like two bows he formed and shaped them,
Like two bended bows together.

"Give me of your roots, O Tamarack!
Of your fibrous roots, O Larch Tree!
My canoe to bind together,
So to bind the ends together
That the water may not enter,
That the river may not wet me!"

And the Larch, with all its fibers,
Shivered in the air of morning,
Touched his forehead with its tassels,
Said, with one long sigh of sorrow,
"Take them all, O Hiawatha!"

From the earth he tore the fibers,
Tore the tough roots of the Larch Tree,
Closely sewed the bark together,
Bound it closely to the framework.

"Give me of your balm, O Fir Tree!
Of your balsam and your resin,
So to close the seams together
That the water may not enter,
That the river may not wet me!"

And the Fir Tree, tall and somber,
Sobbed through all its robes of darkness,
Rattled like a shore with pebbles,
Answered wailing, answered weeping,
"Take my balm, O Hiawatha!"
And he took the tears of balsam,
Took the resin of the Fir Tree,
Smeared therewith each seam and fissure,
Made each crevice safe from water.

Thus the Birch Canoe was builded
In the valley, by the river,
In the bosom of the forest;
And the forest's life was in it,
All its mystery and its magic,
All the lightness of the birch tree,
All the toughness of the cedar,
All the larch's supple sinews;
And it floated on the river
Like a yellow leaf in Autumn,
Like a yellow water lily.

THE OAK FAMILY

Jove's own tree,
That holds the woods in awful sovereignty;
For length of ages lasts his happy reign,
And lives of mortal men contend in vain.
Full in the midst of his own strength he stands,
Stretching his brawny arms and leafy hands;
His shade protects the plains, his head the hills commands.

Vergil.

THE LEGEND OF THE OAK

The oak appears early to have been an object of worship among the Celts and ancient Britons. Under the form of this tree the Celts worshiped their god Tuet, and the Britons Tarnawa, their god of thunder. Baal, the Celtic god of fire, whose festival (that of Yule) was kept at Christmas, was also worshiped under the semblance of an oak. The Druids professed to maintain perpetual fire; and once every year all the fires belonging to the people were extinguished, and relighted from the sacred fire of their priests. This was the origin of the Yule log, with which, even so lately as the middle of the last century, the Christmas fire, in some parts of the country, was always kindled; a fresh log being thrown on and lighted, but taken off before it was consumed, and reserved to kindle the Christmas fire of the following year. The Yule log was always of oak; and as the ancient Britons believed that it was essential for their hearth fires to be renewed every year from the sacred fires of the Druids, so their

A YOUNG OAK

descendants thought that some misfortune would befall them if any accident happened to the Yule log.

The worship of the Druids was generally performed under an oak, and a heap of stones, or cairn, was erected on which the sacred fire was kindled. Before

THE LEGEND OF THE OAK

the ceremony of gathering the mistletoe, the Druids fasted for several days and offered sacrifices in wicker baskets or frames, which, however, were not of willow but of oak twigs curiously interwoven, and were similar to that still carried by Jack-in-the-green on May Day, which, according to some, is a relic of Druidism. The well-known chorus of "Hey, derry down," according to Professor Burnet, was a Druidic chant, signifying literally "In a circle the oak move around."

Criminals were tried under an oak tree; the judge, with the jury, was seated under its shade, and the culprit placed in a circle made by the chief Druid's wand. The Saxons also held their national meetings under an oak; and the celebrated conference between the Saxons and the Britons, after the invasion of the former, was held under the oaks of Dartmoor.

From Loudon's *The Trees and Shrubs of Great Britain*.

THE OAK

JAMES RUSSELL LOWELL

[Near the Beaver Brook Reservation of Boston's park system are the "Waverley Oaks," to the largest of which this poem is addressed. Professor Agassiz said that these trees, some of which were eight hundred years old, had no superior in age on this continent.]

WHAT gnarlèd stretch, what depth of shade, is his!
  There needs no crown to mark the forest's king;
How in his leaves outshines full summer's bliss!
  Sun, storm, rain, dew, to him their tribute bring,
Which he with such benignant royalty
  Accepts, as overpayeth what is lent;
All nature seems his vassal proud to be,
  And cunning only for his ornament.
How towers he, too, amid the billowed snows,
  An unquelled exile from the summer's throne,
Whose plain, uncinctured front more kingly shows,
  Now that the obscuring courtier leaves are flown.
His boughs make music of the winter air,
  Jeweled with sleet, like some cathedral front
Where clinging snowflakes with quaint art repair
  The dints and furrows of time's envious brunt.

THE OAK

How doth his patient strength the rude March wind
    Persuade to seem glad breaths of summer breeze,
And win the soil that fain would be unkind,
    To swell his revenues with proud increase!
He is the gem; and all the landscape wide
    (So doth his grandeur isolate the sense)
Seems but the setting, worthless all beside,
    An empty socket, were he fallen thence.
So, from oft converse with life's wintry gales,
    Should man learn how to clasp with tougher roots
The inspiring earth; how otherwise avails
    The leaf-creating sap that sunward shoots?
So every year that falls with noiseless flake
    Should fill old scars up on the stormward side,
And make hoar age revered for age's sake,
    Not for traditions of youth's leafy pride.
So, from the pinched soil of a churlish fate,
    True hearts compel the sap of sturdier growth,
So between earth and heaven stand simply great,
    That these shall seem but their attendants both;
For nature's forces with obedient zeal
    Wait on the rooted faith and oaken will;
As quickly the pretender's cheat they feel,
    And turn mad Pucks to flout and mock him still.

Lord! all thy works are lessons; each contains
    Some emblem of man's all-containing soul;
Shall he make fruitless all thy glorious pains,
    Delving within thy grace an eyeless mole?
Make me the least of thy Dodona-grove,
    Cause me some message of thy truth to bring,
Speak but a word through me, nor let thy love
    Among my boughs disdain to perch and sing.

THE BOWDOIN OAK

FRANCES L. MACE

Planted in 1802 by George Thorndike, a member of the first class of Bowdoin. He died at the age of twenty-one, the only one of that class remembered by the students of Bowdoin to-day.

Oration of T. R. SIMONTON.

YE breezy boughs of Bowdoin's oak,
  Sing low your summer rune!
In murmuring, rhythmic tones respond
  To every breath of June;

And memories of the joyous youth,
  Through all your songs repeat,
Who plucked the acorn from the twig
  Blown lightly to his feet,

And gayly to his fellows cried:
  "My destiny behold!
This seed shall keep my memory green
  In ages yet untold.

"I trust it to the sheltering sod,
　I hail the promised tree!
Sing, unborn oak, through long decades,
　And ever sing of me!"

By cloud and sunbeam nourished well,
　The tender sapling grew,
Less stalwart than the rose which drank
　From the same cup of dew.

But royal blood was in its veins,
　Of true Hellenic line,
And sunward reached its longing arms
　With impulses divine.

The rushing river as it passed
　Caught whispers from the tree,
And each returning tide brought back
　The answer of the sea.

Till to the listening groves a voice,
　New and harmonious, spoke,
And from a throne of foliage looked
　The spirit of the oak!

THE BOWDOIN OAK

Then birds of happiest omen built
   High in its denser shade,
And grand responses to the storms
   The sounding branches made.

Beneath its bower the bard beloved
   His budding chaplet wore,
The wizard king of romance dreamed
   His wild, enchanting lore;

And scholars, musing in its shade,
   Here heard their country's cry —
Their lips gave back — "Oh, sweet it is
   For native land to die!"

With hearts that burned they cast aside
   These peaceful, oaken bays;
The hero's blood-red path they trod —
   Be theirs the hero's praise.

Oh, though Dodona's voice is hushed,
   A new, intenser flame
Stirs the proud oak to whisper still
   Some dear, illustrious name!

And what of him whose happy mood
   Foretold this sylvan birth?
In boyhood's prime he sank to rest;
   His work was done on earth.

Brief was his race, and light his task
   For immortality,
His only tribute to the years
   The planting of a tree.

Sing low, green oak, thy summer rune,
   Sing valor, love, and truth,
Thyself a fair, embodied thought,
   A living dream of youth.

RHŒCUS

[ABRIDGED]

JAMES RUSSELL LOWELL

The very trees in the forest and along the roadside were supposed to be each under the protection of a special divinity called Hamadryad, said to live and die with the tree intrusted to her care. — GUERBER.

HEAR now this fairy legend of old Greece,
As full of gracious youth and beauty still
As the immortal freshness of that grace
Carved for all ages on some Attic frieze.

A youth named Rhœcus, wandering in the wood,
Saw an old oak just trembling to its fall,
And, feeling pity of so fair a tree,
He propped its gray trunk with admiring care,
And with a thoughtless footstep loitered on.
But, as he turned, he heard a voice behind
That murmured "Rhœcus!" 'T was as if the leaves,
Stirred by a passing breath, had murmured it,
And while he paused bewildered, yet again
It murmured "Rhœcus!" softer than a breeze.

He started and beheld with dizzy eyes
What seemed the substance of a happy dream
Stand there before him, spreading a warm glow
Within the green glooms of the shadowy oak.
It seemed a woman's shape, yet far too fair
To be a woman, and with eyes too meek
For any that were wont to mate with gods.
"Rhœcus, I am the Dryad of this tree,"
Thus she began, dropping her low-toned words
Serene, and full, and clear, as drops of dew,
"And with it I am doomed to live and die;
The rain and sunshine are my caterers,
Nor have I other bliss than simple life;
Now ask me what thou wilt, that I can give,
And with a thankful joy it shall be thine."

Then Rhœcus, with a flutter at the heart,
Yet, by the prompting of such beauty, bold,
Answered: "What is there that can satisfy
The endless craving of the soul but love?
Give me thy love, or but the hope of that
Which must be evermore my nature's goal."
After a little pause she said again,
But with a glimpse of sadness in her tone,

"I give it, Rhœcus, though a perilous gift;
An hour before the sunset meet me here."
And straightway there was nothing he could see
But the green glooms beneath the shadowy oak,
And not a sound came to his straining ears
But the low trickling rustle of the leaves,
And far away upon an emerald slope
The falter of an idle shepherd's pipe.

Now, in those days of simpleness and faith,
Men did not think that happy things were dreams
Because they overstepped the narrow bourn
Of likelihood, but reverently deemed
Nothing too wondrous or too beautiful
To be the guerdon of a daring heart.
So Rhœcus made no doubt that he was blest,
And all along unto the city's gate
Earth seemed to spring beneath him as he walked,
The clear, broad sky looked bluer than its wont,
And he could scarce believe he had not wings,
Such sunshine seemed to glitter through his veins
Instead of blood, so light he felt and strange.

Young Rhœcus had a faithful heart enough,
But one that in the present dwelt too much,

And, taking with blithe welcome whatsoe'er
Chance gave of joy, was wholly bound in that,
Like the contented peasant of a vale,
Deemed it the world, and never looked beyond.
So, haply meeting in the afternoon
Some comrades who were playing at the dice,
He joined them and forgot all else beside.

The dice were rattling at the merriest,
And Rhœcus, who had met but sorry luck,
Just laughed in triumph at a happy throw,
When through the room there hummed a yellow bee
That buzzed about his ear with down-dropped legs
As if to light. And Rhœcus laughed and said,
Feeling how red and flushed he was with loss,
"By Venus! does he take me for a rose?"
And brushed him off with rough, impatient hand.
But still the bee came back, and thrice again
Rhœcus did beat him off with growing wrath.
Then through the window flew the wounded bee,
And Rhœcus, tracking him with angry eyes,
Saw a sharp mountain peak of Thessaly
Against the red disk of the setting sun,—
And instantly the blood sank from his heart,

RHŒCUS

As if its very walls had caved away.
Without a word he turned, and, rushing forth,
Ran madly through the city and the gate,
And o'er the plain, which now the wood's long shade,
By the low sun thrown forward broad and dim,
Darkened wellnigh unto the city's wall.

Quite spent and out of breath he reached the tree,
And, listening fearfully, he heard once more
The low voice murmur "Rhœcus!" close at hand:
Whereat he looked around him, but could see
Naught but the deepening glooms beneath the oak.
Then sighed the voice, "O Rhœcus! nevermore
Shalt thou behold me or by day or night,
Me, who would fain have blessed thee with a love
More ripe and bounteous than ever yet
Filled up with nectar any mortal heart:
But thou didst scorn my humble messenger,
And sent'st him back to me with bruisèd wings.
We spirits only show to gentle eyes,
We ever ask an undivided love,
And he who scorns the least of Nature's works
Is thenceforth exiled and shut out from all.
Farewell! for thou canst never see me more."

THE BEECH FAMILY

THERE, at the foot of yonder nodding beech
That wreathes its old fantastic roots so high —

THOMAS GRAY.

IN THE SHADOW OF THE BEECHES

MADISON J. CAWEIN

In the shadow of the beeches,
  Where the many wild flowers bloom,
Where the leafy silence pleaches
  Green a roof of cool perfume,
    Have you felt an awe imperious
    As when, in a church mysterious,
  Windows fill with God the gloom?

In the shadow of the beeches,
  Where the rock-ledged waters flow,
Where the sun's white splendor bleaches
  Every wave to foaming snow,
    Have you felt a music solemn
    As when minster arch and column
  Echo organ worship low?

In the shadow of the beeches,
  Where the light and shade are blent,
Where the forest bird beseeches,

FRUITING SPRAY OF BEECH

And the wild is sweet with scent —
  Is it joy or melancholy
  That o'erwhelms us partly, wholly
To our spirit's betterment?

In the shadow of the beeches
  Lay me where no eye perceives;
Where — like some great arm that reaches
  Gently as a love that grieves —
    One gnarled root may clasp me kindly;
    While the long years, working blindly,
  Slowly change my dust to leaves.

Reprinted from the *New York Independent*.

THE BEECH TREE'S PETITION

THOMAS CAMPBELL

Oh, leave this barren spot to me!
Spare, woodman, spare the beechen tree!
Though bush or flow'ret never grow
My dark, unwarming shade below;
Nor summer bud perfume the dew
Of rosy blush, or yellow hue;
Nor fruits of autumn, blossom-born,
My green and glassy leaves adorn;
Nor murmuring tribes from me derive
Th' ambrosial amber of the hive;
Yet leave this barren spot to me:
Spare, woodman, spare the beechen tree!

Thrice twenty summers I have seen
The sky grow bright, the forest green;
And many a wintry wind have stood
In bloomless, fruitless solitude,
Since childhood in my pleasant bower
First spent its sweet and sportive hour,

Since youthful lovers in my shade
Their vows of truth and rapture made,
And on my trunk's surviving frame
Carved many a long-forgotten name.
Oh! by the sighs of gentle sound,
First breathed upon this sacred ground;
By all that Love has whispered here,
Or Beauty heard with ravished ear;
As Love's own altar honor me:
Spare, woodman, spare the beechen tree!

THE WILLOW FAMILY

    I. WILLOW
   II. ASPEN
  III. POPLAR

Willows whiten, aspens quiver,
Little breezes dusk and shiver.

Tennyson.

UNDER THE WILLOWS

[ABRIDGED]

JAMES RUSSELL LOWELL

[Reference is here made to an ancient group of seven willows near the Charles River, of which six, as in the poet's time, are standing. They are found, three on each side of Mt. Auburn Street, Cambridge, and the largest is the one especially described in the poem.]

I CARE not how men trace their ancestry,
To ape or Adam; let them please their whim;
But I in June am midway to believe
A tree among my far progenitors,
Such sympathy is mine with all the race,
Such mutual recognition vaguely sweet
There is between us. Surely there are times
When they consent to own me of their kin,
And condescend to me, and call me cousin,
Murmuring faint lullabies of eldest time,
Forgotten, and yet dumbly felt with thrills
Moving the lips, though fruitless of all words.
And I have many a lifelong leafy friend,
That knows I hate the ax, and welcomes me
Within his tent as if I were a bird,

Or other free companion of the earth,
Yet undegenerate to the shifts of men.
Among them one, an ancient willow, spreads
Eight balanced limbs, springing at once all round,
His deep-ridged trunk with upward slant diverse,
In outline like enormous beaker, fit
For hand of Jotun, where 'mid snow and mist
He holds unwieldy revel. This tree, spared,
I know not by what grace, — for in the blood
Of our New World subduers lingers yet
Hereditary feud with trees, they being
(They and the red man most) our fathers' foes, —
Is one of six, a willow Pleiades,
The seventh fallen, that lean along the brink
Where the steep upland dips into the marsh,
Their roots, like molten metal cooled in flowing,
Stiffened in coils and runnels down the bank.
The friend of all the winds, wide-armed he towers
And glints his steely aglets in the sun,
Or whitens fitfully with sudden bloom
Of leaves breeze-lifted, much as when a shoal
Of devious minnows wheel from where a pike
Lurks balanced 'neath the lily pads, and whirl
A rood of silver bellies to the day.

THE ASPEN

BERNHARD SEVERIN INGEMANN

WHAT whispers so strange, at the hour of midnight,
    From the aspen's leaves trembling so wildly?
Why in the lone wood sings it sad, when the bright
    Full moon beams upon it so mildly?

It soundeth as 'mid the harp strings the wind gust,
    Or like sighs of ghosts wandering in sorrow;
In the meadow the small flowers hear it, and must
    With tears close themselves till the morrow.

"Oh, tell me, poor wretch, why thou shiverest so, —
    Why the moans of distraction thou pourest;
Say, can thy heart harbor repentance and woe?
    Can sin reach the child of the forest?"

"Yes," sighed forth the tremulous voice, — "for thy race
    Has not alone fallen from its station;
Not alone art thou seeking for comfort and grace,
    Nor alone art thou called to salvation.

"I've heard, too, the voice, which, with heaven reconciled,
  The earth to destruction devoted;
But the storm from my happiness hurried me wild
  Though round me joy's melodies floated.

" By Kedron I stood, and the bright beaming eye
  I viewed of the pitying Power;
Each tree bowed its head, as the Savior passed by,
  But I deigned not my proud head to lower.

"I towered to the cloud, whilst the lilies sang sweet,
  And the rose bent its stem in devotion;
I strewed not my leaves 'fore the Holy One's feet,
  Nor bough nor twig set I in motion.

"Then sounded a sigh from the Savior's breast;
  And I quaked, for that sigh through me darted;
'Quake so till I come!' said the voice of the Blest;
  My repose then forever departed.

" And now must I tremble by night and by day,
  For me there no moment of ease is;
I must sigh with regret in such dolorous way,
  Whilst each floweret can smile when it pleases.

THE ASPEN 141

"And tremble shall I till the Last Day arrive
    And I view the Redeemer returning;
My sorrow and punishment long will survive,
    Till the world shall in blazes be burning."

So whispers the doomed one at midnight; its tone
    Is that of ghosts wandering in sorrow;
The small flowers hear it within the wood lone
    And with tears close themselves till the morrow.

THE LEGEND OF THE POPLAR

The forest trees slept. The leaves were still. Even the quivering, shivering poplar leaves were quiet, and deep was the hush over the whole forest. Once a sleepy little bird broke the silence by a call to his mate, then all was still again, until nearer and nearer came the cautious footsteps of an old man. He entered the wood and peered carefully in every direction; no one was in sight, and he went farther into the wood. With every step dry leaves rustled, and every now and then a twig crackled. He could see nobody, to be sure, but the noises terrified him. He was startled each time a twig snapped, and he kept looking nervously over his shoulder. Still he saw no one, but his courage rapidly oozed away and soon was entirely gone. Another noise, and he thrust among the thick branches of a poplar tree a heavy round object that he had hugged tight under his cloak. Then he turned and hurried out of the wood as fast as his stiff old limbs could carry him. Not a tree woke, and only the old man himself knew what was hidden in the poplar tree.

Lombardy Poplars

The next morning the trees awoke to see a most beautiful day dawning. Only the afternoon before a shower had washed all nature bright, and it seemed this fair morning as if some of the beautiful rainbow tints still lingered in the air. The poplar was shaking a few last drops from its leaves and looking proudly at the shade it cast — for the thick branches of the poplar were straight branches in those days — when a cry went ringing through the forest.

It was the voice of Iris, beautiful goddess of the rainbow.

"The pot of gold at the foot of the rainbow has been stolen! Stolen! Know you anything of it?"

The trees all shook their heads in denial. Who would be so base as to steal the pot of gold from Iris? Not they.

On sped Iris in her rainbow colors to seek Father Jupiter. She told him the calamity, and the anger of the ruler of the universe was kindled.

"We will find its hiding place, my daughter," he said; and straightway the eyes of Jupiter were turned from the sights of Olympus to those of Earth.

"Who knows the hiding place of the pot of gold?" thundered Jupiter.

THE LEGEND OF THE POPLAR 145

"Not I, not I, not I!" chorused the trees.

"Lift up your branches to show you speak the truth," commanded the mighty Jupiter, and lo! to the surprise of every tree and to the poplar most of all, from the branches of the poplar tree fell the treasure. Scornfully all the other trees looked on the poplar, and the poor poplar shivered and trembled. Soon, however, the poplar straightened and stiffened.

"Never again," it solemnly said, "shall my thick branches shelter the stolen goods of others; always, hereafter, shall my branches point straight to heaven to declare my innocence and to signify my truthfulness."

Long, long ago this happened, but the arms of the poplar are upraised even to this day.

THE SISTERS OF PHAËTHON

[Phaëthon, the son of Apollo, obtained his father's permission to drive for one day the chariot of the sun through the heavens. But he was unable to guide the horses, and the world was set on fire. Jupiter hurled a thunderbolt at Phaëthon, which caused him to fall lifeless into the Po. The sisters of Phaëthon, for their persistent grief, were changed into poplar trees.]

THE daughters of the Sun, lamenting sore,
Cease not to mourn the brother they have lost.
To him though dead they bring their empty gifts —
The tears and sighs that untoward sorrow prompts.
They prostrate kneel before his burial place,
And night and day they call on Phaëthon,
Who cannot hear their loud, ungoverned grief.
Four times the crescent moon had joined her horns,
Yet all the while their loud lament they made
In their accustomed way; for grief had grown,
From long indulgence, to a habit fixed.
And last, as Phaëthusa, eldest born
Of all the sisters, sought to cast herself
In unrestrained emotion on the earth,
She felt her feet grow stiff and motionless;
And when Lampetie, the shining one,

Would fain have hastened to her sister's aid
Her willing feet a sudden root detained.
The other sister, filled with deep concern,
In token of her grief would tear her hair,
But only leaves, alas! her fingers plucked.
And now aghast one feels her rigid limbs
Incased within a slowly rising trunk;
Another, horror-struck, beholds her arms,
Outstretched in aid, to leafy boughs extend.
And while they marvel at the sight, the bark,
With gradual growth, steals o'er their bodies all:
It hides their shoulders and their heads; their mouths
Alone remain to speak their wretched woe,
And call their mother to their piteous plight.
What can the mother do? What more than rush
This way and that, as frenzied grief impels,
And while there yet is time — in frantic haste —
Press hurried kisses on their stiffening lips?
'T is not enough, and in despair she strives
To tear their bodies from the cruel trunk.
With eager haste she breaks the tender shoots,
But drops of blood, as from a wound, flow forth —
"Oh, spare me, mother!" each one wounded cries;
"Forbear, I pray! For when the bark is rent,

My body thou dost tear within the tree.
And now farewell!" No other words they speak,
For now the bark, grown wholly o'er their mouths,
Has checked their speech. Then copious tears they shed,
That, flowing ceaselessly from out the tree,
And, hardening when the sunlight touches them,
At length to lustrous amber are transformed.
Those precious tears the glistening Po receives
And sends them to be worn as ornaments
By daughters of the noble Latin homes.

From OVID's *Metamorphoses*.

THE PINE FAMILY

    I. PINE
   II. FIR
  III. HEMLOCK

This is the forest primeval. The murmuring pines and the hemlocks,
Bearded with moss, and in garments green, indistinct in the twilight,
Stand like Druids of eld, with voices sad and prophetic,
Stand like harpers hoar, with beards that rest on their bosoms.

                                                        LONGFELLOW.

A SONG

Away on a northern mountain
    A lonely pine is found;
A mantle of white infolds him,
    And ice and snow surround.

He dreams of a distant palm tree,
    That, far in the southern land,
Keepeth a sorrowful silence,
    Alone, 'mid the burning sand.

Translated from Heine.

PINE TREES

JOHN RUSKIN

THE pine is trained to need nothing and to endure everything. Tall or short, it will be straight. Small or large, it will be round. It may be permitted to the soft, lowland trees that they should make themselves gay with the show of blossom and glad with the pretty charities of fruitfulness. We builders with the sword have harder work to do for man, and must do it in close-set troops.

To stay the sliding of the mountain snows, which would bury him; to hold in divided drops, at our sword points, the rain, which would sweep away him and his treasure fields; to nurse in shade among our brown, fallen leaves the tricklings that feed the brooks in drought; to give massive shield against the winter wind, which shrieks through the bare branches of the plain, — such service must we do him steadfastly while we live.

Our bodies also are at his service; softer than the bodies of other trees, though our service is harder than

A WHITE PINE

theirs. Let him take them as he pleases for his houses and ships. So also it may be well for these timid, lowland trees to tremble with all their leaves, or turn their paleness to the sky, if but a rush of rain passes by them; or to let fall their leaves at last, sick and sere. But we pines must live amidst the wrath of clouds.

We only wave our branches to and fro when the storm pleads with us, as men toss their arms in a dream.

And, finally, these weak, lowland trees may struggle fondly for the last remnant of life, and send up feeble saplings again from their roots when they are cut down. But we builders with the sword perish boldly; our dying shall be perfect and solemn, as our warring; we give up our lives without reluctance, and forever.

I wish the reader to fix his attention for a moment on these two great characters of the pine, its straightness and rounded perfectness; both wonderful, and in their issue lovely. I say first its straightness. Because we see it in the wildest scenery, we are apt to remember only as examples of it those which have been disturbed by violent accident or disease. Of course such instances are frequent. The soil of the pine is subject to continual change; perhaps the rock in which it is rooted splits in frost and falls forward, throwing the young stems aslope, or the whole mass of earth around it is undermined by rain, or a huge bowlder falls on its stem from above and forces it for twenty years to grow with the weight of several tons leaning on its side.

Nevertheless this is not the truest or universal expression of the pine's character. The pine rises in serene resistance, self-contained; nor can I ever without awe stay long under a great Alpine cliff, looking up to its great companies of pine.

You cannot reach them; those trees never heard human voice; they are far above all sound but that of the winds. No foot ever stirred fallen leaf of theirs.

Then note, farther, their perfectness. The pine stands compact, like one of its own cones, slightly curved on its sides, and, instead of being wild in its expression, forms the softest of all forest scenery. For other trees show their trunks and twisting boughs; but the pine, growing either in luxuriant mass or in happy isolation, allows no bough to be seen. Lowland forests arch overhead and checker the ground with darkness; but the pine, growing in scattered groups, leaves the glades between emerald bright. Its gloom is all its own; narrowing to the sky, it lets the sunshine strike down to the dew.

And then I want you to notice in the pine its exquisite fineness. Other trees rise against the sky in dots and knots, but this in fringes.

You never see the edges of it, so subtle are they; and for this reason it alone of trees, so far as I know, is capable of the fiery changes noticed by Shakespeare.

When the sun rises behind a ridge crested with pine, provided the ridge be at a distance of about two miles, and seen clear, all the trees for about three or four degrees on each side of the sun become trees of light, seen in clear flame against the darker sky, and dazzling as the sun itself.

I thought at first this was owing to the actual luster of the leaves; but I believe now it is caused by the cloud dew upon them, every minutest leaf carrying its diamond. It seems as if these trees, living always among the clouds, had caught part of their glory from them.

From *Modern Painters*.

I REMEMBER, I REMEMBER

THOMAS HOOD

I REMEMBER, I remember
The fir trees dark and high;
I used to think their slender tops
Were close against the sky:
It was a childish ignorance,
But now 'tis little joy
To know I'm farther off from heaven
Than when I was a boy.

A YOUNG FIR WOOD

DANTE GABRIEL ROSSETTI

These little firs to-day are things
   To clasp into a giant's cap,
   Or fans to suit his lady's lap.
From many winters many springs
   Shall cherish them in strength and sap,
   Till they be marked upon the map,
A wood for the wind's wanderings.

All seed is in the sower's hands:
   And what at first was trained to spread
   Its shelter for some single head,—
Yea, even such fellowship of wands,—
   May hide the sunset, and the shade
   Of its great multitude be laid
Upon the earth and elder sands.

THE HEMLOCK TREE

HENRY WADSWORTH LONGFELLOW

O HEMLOCK tree! O hemlock tree! how faithful
    are thy branches!
  Green not alone in summer time,
  But in the winter's frost and rime!
O hemlock tree! O hemlock tree! how faithful
    are thy branches!

MISCELLANEOUS SELECTIONS

TREES IN WINTER

WINTER LEAFAGE

EDITH M. THOMAS

Each year I mark one lone outstanding tree,
Clad in its robings of the summer past,
Dry, wan, and shivering in the wintry blast.
It will not pay the season's rightful fee,—
It will not set its frost-burnt leafage free;
But like some palsied miser all aghast,
Who hoards his sordid treasure to the last,
It sighs, it moans, it sings in eldritch glee,
A foolish tree, to dote on summer gone;
A faithless tree, that never feels how spring
Creeps up the world to make a leafy dawn,
And recompense for all despoilment brings.
Oh, let me not, heyday and youth withdrawn,
With failing hands to their vain semblance cling!

A PROTEST AGAINST FELLING THE TREES

WILLIAM WORDSWORTH

I FEEL at times a motion of despite
Towards one, whose bold contrivances and skill,
As you have seen, bear such conspicuous part
In works of havoc; taking from these vales,
One after one, their proudest ornaments.
Full oft his doings lead me to deplore
Tall ash tree sown by winds, by vapors nursed,
In the dry crannies of the pendent rocks;
Light birch aloft upon the horizon's edge,
A veil of glory for the ascending moon;
And oak whose roots by noontide dew were damped,
And on whose forehead inaccessible
The raven lodged in safety. Many a ship
Launched into Morecamb Bay, to him hath owed
Her strong knee timbers, and the mast that bears
The loftiest of her pendants; he, from park
Or forest, fetched the enormous axle-tree
That whirls (how slow itself!) ten thousand spindles.
And the vast engine laboring in the mine,

Content with meaner prowess, must have lacked
The trunk and body of its marvelous strength,
If his undaunted enterprise had failed
Among the mountain coves.

      Yon household fir,
A guardian planted to fence off the blast,
But towering high the roof above, as if
Its humble destination were forgot; —
That sycamore, which annually holds
Within its shade, as in a stately tent
On all sides open to the fanning breeze,
A grave assemblage, seated while they shear
The fleece-encumbered flock; — the joyful elm,
Around whose trunk the maidens dance in May; —
And the Lord's oak; — would plead their several rights
In vain, if he were master of their fate;
His sentence to the ax would doom them all.

From *The Excursion*.

CHARACTERISTICS OF THE TREES

AND foorth they passe with pleasure forward led,
Joying to heare the birdes sweete harmony,
Which therein shrouded from the tempest dred,
Seemed in their song to scorn the cruell sky.
Much can they praise the trees so straight and hy,
The sayling Pine; the Cedar proud and tall;
The vine-propp Elm; the Poplar never dry;
The builder Oake, sole king of forrests all;
The Aspen good for staves; the Cypresse funerall;
The Laurel, meed of mightie conquerours
And poets sage; the Firre that weepeth still;
The Eugh, obedient to the bender's will;
The Birch, for shafts; the Sallow for the mill;
The Mirrhe sweete-bleeding in the bitter wound;
The warlike Beech; the Ash for nothing ill;
The fruitfull Olive; and the Platane round;
The carven Holme; the Maple seldom inward sound.

From SPENSER'S *The Faerie Queene*, Book I, canto i.

AMPHION

ALFRED TENNYSON

Amphion was one of the most famous of mythical musicians. Having become king of Thebes, it is said that when he played on his lyre, stones moved of their own accord, and took their places in the wall while he was fortifying the city. — GAYLEY'S *Classic Myths*.

My father left a park to me,
 But it is wild and barren,
A garden too with scarce a tree,
 And waster than a warren:
Yet say the neighbors when they call,
 It is not bad but good land,
And in it is the germ of all
 That grows within the woodland.

Oh, had I lived when song was great
 In days of old Amphion,
And ta'en my fiddle to the gate,
 Nor cared for seed or scion!
And had I lived when song was great,
 And legs of trees were limber,

And ta'en my fiddle to the gate,
　And fiddled in the timber!

'T is said he had a tuneful tongue,
　Such happy intonation,
Wherever he sat down and sung
　He left a small plantation;
Wherever in a lonely grove
　He set up his forlorn pipes,
The gouty oak began to move,
　And flounder into hornpipes.

The mountain stirr'd its bushy crown,
　And, as tradition teaches,
Young ashes pirouetted down
　Coquetting with young beeches;
And briony-vine and ivy-wreath
　Ran forward to his rhyming,
And from the valleys underneath
　Came little copses climbing.

The linden broke her ranks and rent
　The woodbine wreaths that bind her,
And down the middle buzz! she went
　With all her bees behind her;

The poplars, in long order due,
  With cypress promenaded,
The shock-head willows two and two
  By rivers gallopaded.

Came wet-shot alder from the wave,
  Came yews, a dismal coterie;
Each pluck'd his one foot from the grave,
  Poussetting with a sloe tree;
Old elms came breaking from the vine,
  The vine stream'd out to follow,
And, sweating rosin, plump'd the pine
  From many a cloudy hollow.

And wasn't it a sight to see,
  When, ere his song was ended,
Like some great landslip, tree by tree,
  The countryside descended;
And shepherds from the mountain eaves
  Look'd down, half-pleased, half-frighten'd,
As dash'd about the drunken leaves
  The random sunshine lighten'd?

THE PALM TREE

JOHN GREENLEAF WHITTIER

Is it the palm, the cocoa palm,
On the Indian Sea, by the isles of balm?
Or is it a ship in the breezeless calm?

A ship whose keel is of palm beneath,
Whose ribs of palm have a palm-bark sheath,
And a rudder of palm it steereth with.

Branches of palm are its spars and rails,
Fibers of palm are its woven sails,
And the rope is of palm that idly trails!

What does the good ship bear so well?
The cocoanut with its stony shell,
And the milky sap of its inner cell.

What are its jars, so smooth and fine,
But hollowed nuts, filled with oil and wine,
And the cabbage that ripens under the Line?

Who smokes his nargileh, cool and calm?
The master, whose cunning and skill could charm
Cargo and ship from the bounteous palm.

In the cabin he sits on a palm mat soft,
From a beaker of palm his drink is quaffed,
And a palm thatch shields from the sun aloft!

His dress is woven of palmy strands,
And he holds a palm-leaf scroll in his hands,
Traced with the Prophet's wise commands!

The turban folded about his head
Was daintily wrought of the palm-leaf braid,
And the fan that cools him of palm was made.

Of threads of palm was the carpet spun
Whereon he kneels when the day is done,
And the foreheads of Islam are bowed as one!

To him the palm is a gift divine,
Wherein all uses of man combine, —
House, and raiment, and food, and wine!

And, in the hour of his great release,
His need of the palm shall only cease
With the shroud wherein he lieth in peace.

"Allah il Allah!" he sings his psalm,
On the Indian Sea, by the isles of balm;
"Thanks to Allah who gives the palm!"

GENERAL OUTLINE FOR THE STUDY OF TREES

GENERAL CHARACTERISTICS:
  Locality.
  Height.
  Growth.
  Form of top.
  Evergreen or deciduous.

ROOTS:
  Size.
  Direction.

TRUNK:
  Circumference.
  Bark.
    Color.
    Surface.
    Use.
  Wood.
    Use.

BRANCHES:
  Height of lowest.
  Angle with trunk.
  Color and surface of branchlets.

WINTER BUDS:
  Arrangement.
  Form.
  Size.
  Surface.
  Color.

LEAVES:
  Time of appearing.
  Color.
  Size.
  Arrangement.
  Division.
  Shape.
    General outline.
    Ratio of length and width.
    Margin.
    Base.
    Apex.
  Venation.
  Surface.
  Attachment.

FLOWERS:
  Time of appearing.

FLOWERS (*continued*):
  Size and color.
  Arrangement.
  Parts.

    (*a*) Calyx.
        Color.
        Sepals.

    (*b*) Corolla.
        Color.
        Petals.

    (*c*) Stamens.
        Number.
        Parts.

    (*d*) Pistils.
        Number.
  Fragrance.

FRUIT:
  Kind.
  Period of growth.
  Description.
  Use.

HISTORY:
  Connection with important events.

HISTORICAL AMERICAN TREES

1. The Big Tree of Geneseo, New York.
2. The Charter Oak, Hartford, Conn.
3. Penn's Treaty Tree, Philadelphia.
4. The Stuyvesant Pear Tree, New York.
5. Gates's Weeping Willow, New York.
6. Pontiac's Memorial Tree, Detroit.
7. The Washington Elm, Cambridge.
8. The Tory Tulip Tree, King's Mountain.
9. The Jane M'Crea Tree, Fort Edward.
10. The Balm of Gilead Tree, Fort Edward.
11. The Magnolia Council Tree, Charleston, S.C.
12. Wayne's Black Walnut, near Stony Point, N.Y.
13. Arnold's Willow, near West Point.
14. The Rhode Island Sycamore, near the Seaconnet.
15. The Washington Cypress, Dismal Swamp.
16. The Miami Apple Tree, opposite Fort Wayne.
17. Villere's Pecan Tree, near New Orleans.
18. The Fox Oak, Flushing, Long Island.

    For account of 1–18, see *Harper's Magazine*, May, 1862.

19. The Eliot Oak.

    For account of above, see the *Bay State Monthly*, Vol. I, p. 84.

20. The Monarch, Boston Common.
21. The Liberty Tree, Boston.

22. The Second Liberty Tree, Quincy, Mass.
23. The Hangman's Tree, Quincy.

> For account of 20–23, see *New England Magazine*, July, 1900.

24. The Whittemore Elm.
25. The Groom Willow.

> For account of 24 and 25, see L. L. Dame's *Typical Trees of Massachusetts*.

SUPPLEMENTARY READING

A Ballad of Trees and the Master	*Sidney Lanier.*
Apples in the Cellar	*J. G. Holland.*
Eliot's Oak	*L. L. Dame.*
Eliot's Oak	*Henry Wadsworth Longfellow.*
March	*Helen Hunt Jackson.*
My Hickory Fire	*Helen Hunt Jackson.*
Nutting	*William Wordsworth.*
Selections from Cowley's "The Garden."	
September Woods	*Helen Hunt Jackson.*
The Arab to the Palm	*Bayard Taylor.*
The Elms of New Haven	*Nathaniel P. Willis.*
The Marshes of Glynn	*Sidney Lanier.*
The Rowan Tree	*Lady Nairne.*
The Smoking Pine	*Emma Huntington Nason.*
The Spice Tree	*John Stirling.*
The Tree	*Bjornstjerne Björnson.*
The Tree	*Jones Very.*
The Weeping Willow	*Elizabeth Akers Allen.*
The Wonderful One-Hoss Shay	*Oliver Wendell Holmes.*
The Yellow Elms	*Bessie Chandler.*
Wild Apples	*Henry David Thoreau.*
Woodman! Spare that Tree	*George P. Morris.*

NOTES

(Heavy-faced figures refer to pages)

7. Wood-nymphs. Wood-nymphs, or Dryads, one of several classes of nymphs. Others were Oreads, nymphs of mountains and grottoes, and Naiads, or water-nymphs. Pan, the god of woods and fields, led the dances of the Dryads. See also note, p. 168.

8. Laocoön. A Trojan priest, who, with his two sons, was strangled by twin serpents.

11. Jove, Jupiter, or Zeus, king of the gods. His home was "many-peaked" Olympus, and there he assembled the gods for conferences or for feasts. He is represented as a fine, majestic figure; the world is his footstool; and the eagle — emblem of strength and power — is generally seen close beside him.

11. Delphic. An adjective made from Delphi, where Apollo had his most famous oracle.

11. Tenedos, Claros, Patara. Places containing famous temples of Apollo.

11. Fates. Three sisters, Clotho, Lachesis, and Atropos, who controlled human destiny.

11. Archer god. An allusion to Apollo's skill with the bow.

14. Capitol. Triumphal processions in Rome always passed along the Sacra Via, one of the streets which bounded the Forum, and then ascended the Capitol, where the victorious generals offered sacrifice in the Temple of Jupiter.

18. Andersen's melancholy story. See "The Fir Tree" in *The Wonder Stories* of Hans Andersen.

TREES IN PROSE AND POETRY

18. Val St. Veronique. A remarkably fertile valley in southeastern France.

20. Village Blacksmith's Chestnut Tree. This tree, in reality a horse-chestnut tree, was removed by the city of Cambridge when the street in which it stood was widened.

21. The Danish king. Canute, the first Danish king of England, to show his courtiers the emptiness of their extravagant praise, ordered his chair placed on the seashore and commanded the waves to come no farther. When it was seen that his command availed nothing he succeeded in teaching his subjects the worthlessness of their flattery.

35. "**Curly maple,**" prized, like bird's-eye maple, for interior furnishings.

37. Madame Camilla. Refers to Madame Camilla Urso, the famous violinist.

37. Cremona. A town of Italy, famous for its violins.

45. Cintra's vine. Cintra, a town of Portugal, remarkable for the fruitfulness of its soil and for its mild climate. Its scenery is described in Byron's *Childe Harold*.

70. Surtur. "A giant of mythology who is to set the world on fire at the great consummation." (Scandinavian mythology.)

70. Upsala. A reference to Old Upsala or Upsal, the traditional capital of Odin, about three miles north of modern Upsala, in the vicinity of Stockholm.

70. Ditmarsh. A country on the North Sea between the Eider and the Elbe, conquered by the Danes in 1589, and in 1866 annexed to Prussia.

77. The Venerable Bede. The earliest historian of England. His greatest work, *Historia Ecclesiastica*, was translated by King Alfred.

77. Chrysostom. One of the fathers of the early church, and a martyr to his faith.

77. Lepsius. A German Egyptologist.

NOTES 183

86. "**Under the Washington Elm.**" This poem, written at the beginning of the Civil War, emphasizes the fact that the desire for freedom is the same in April, 1861, as at the outbreak of the Revolution in April, 1775.

86. **The south-wind moans.** Referring to the news from the South during the second April.

86. **The murder-haunted town.** This stanza has special reference to the mob attack on the 6th Massachusetts regiment when passing through Baltimore.

88. **Than the army of worms that gnawed below.** The strength of the government was being eaten away by the moral corruption of slavery and by the secession movement of the South.

90. **The great Johnston Elm.** A famous tree near Providence, R.I.

107. **Cheemaun, Taquamenaw.** Indian words signifying respectively a birch canoe, and a river emptying into Lake Superior.

115. **Dartmoor.** A desolate tract of land in Devonshire, England.

117. **Pucks.** See Shakespeare's *Midsummer Night's Dream*.

118. **Dodona-grove.** Dodona, a city of Epirus, which contained the most ancient oracle of Greece. Before the erection of a temple to Zeus the prophecies were given from the branches of an oak, and poets have since commonly ascribed the power of prophetic speech to the oak grove at Dodona.

120. **True Hellenic line.** The Greeks were called Hellenes, from Hellas, the ancient name of their country.

120. **The rushing river.** The Androscoggin.

121. **The bard beloved.** Longfellow.

121. **The wizard king of romance.** Hawthorne.

138. **Jotun.** A mythical Scandinavian giant.

140. **Kedron, or Kidron.** A brook in a ravine under the east wall of Jerusalem, between the city and the Mount of Olives.

165. **Morecamb Bay.** An arm of the Irish Sea, indenting the western coast of England.

167. The eugh (yew), the sallow (a kind of willow), the mirrhe (myrrh), the platane (plane tree), and the holme (ilex) are common in England.

168. When song was great. For similar musical powers read the story of Orpheus and the contest between Apollo and Pan. See also Shelley's *Hymn of Pan*, and Browning's *The Pied Piper of Hamelin*.

169. With all her bees behind her. The bees are specially fond of the linden, or lime tree, and always find the nectar-laden blossoms.

172. The prophet's. Mohammed's.

172. Islam. The whole body of believers in Mohammed.

173. Allah. The Mohammedan name of the Supreme Being.